INSTALLING EXHIBITIONS

A PRACTICAL GUIDE

INSTALLING EXHIBITIONS

A PRACTICAL GUIDE

PETE SMITHSON

First published in 2009 by
A & C Black Publishers Limited
36 Soho Square
London W1D 3QY
www.acblack.com

ISBN: 978-1-408-11016-4

CIP Catalogue records for this book are available from the British Library and the U.S. Library of Congress.

Designer: James Watson
Commissioning Editor: Susan James
Managing Editor: Sophie Page
Copyeditor: Julian Beecroft

This book is produced using paper that is made from wood grown in managed, sustainable forests. It is natural, renewable and recyclable. The logging and manufacturing processes conform to the environmental regulations of the country of origin.

Printed in China by C & C Offset Printing Co Ltd.

contents

ACKNOWLEDGEMENTS

I would like to thank the University of the Arts, London, for the Teaching and Learning Fellowship I was awarded in 2006/7, without which the writing and illustrating of this guide would not have been possible. Also, for further funding from CLIP CETL (Creative Learning in Practice Centre for Excellence in Teaching and Learning), within the University of Arts, London.

I would particularly like to thank the following people: Richard Gough, Jefford Horrigan, Sonia Boyce, Michael Blackett, Vivien Blackett and all my colleagues and friends at Central Saint Martins College of Art and Design, for their help, advice and support.

INTRODUCTION

The first question you should ask yourself is, 'What type of work do I make and how am I intending to show it?' You can make fantastic work, but if it's badly installed you're letting yourself down. The installation should be seen as part of the process of the work, not just something that's tagged onto the end. This way it should become a more meaningful and, hopefully, enjoyable activity.

The purpose of this book is to be a practical guide on how to put up a show or exhibition. It's not about aesthetics or the making of work. It has been written and illustrated to help achieve this task, though it does assume different levels of knowledge.

The first part of the book is universal and will be useful to all. The later sections are more specific to different practices. There is a separate stage on hanging two-dimensional work, but information on the installation of object-based work is contained throughout the guide.

Pete Smithson

1

stage one

considerations
risk assessment
health & safety

notes

CONSIDERATIONS BEFORE INSTALLATION

THE SPACE

This is the first consideration. Think about your work in relation to the space you have to show in. Is it a white cube? Does it have architectural features? What condition is it in? Does it need cleaning and painting? Should you use the space as it is? It's very easy to get preoccupied by preparation, spending days making it immaculate, losing track of your work and consequently leaving no time for installation.

There may be restrictions in a given space. Do not assume a free reign. You will have to negotiate with those responsible and/or other exhibitors. You may have to compromise, but see this as part of the working process, not as a negative. Learning to use space to its best advantage is a skill.

How is the space constructed? For example, are the walls solid brick or lined with ply, chipboard or plasterboard? What is the floor like – is it wooden planks or sheets, painted, concrete, lino? Is the ceiling plasterboard, solid, suspended, etc.? These are important considerations if you need to use any fixing devices, particularly if the work is heavy or suspended.

Do you have sole use of the space? If not, find out what the other people are showing and what they are planning; remember the public look at the show as a whole and not just individual pieces. What's happening in adjacent spaces? Are the spaces light or dark; is there a sound element to your work or to that of others in the vicinity?

ACTION PLAN

notes

Plan your time; think realistically about how long things take. I would always overestimate, and if you finish before schedule – great! Time-manage by splitting the days into different tasks. What equipment/tools/materials are you going to need and where will you get them? Will you need help? Do as much planning as you can before you get into the space. Think about the best time both to order and to take delivery of materials and equipment. If the work is not already on site, when should it be delivered? If extensive painting/site preparation is required, it may be better for the work to be delivered at a later stage.

BUDGET

Showing work can be expensive, so plan ahead and be realistic. Loads of money does not necessarily mean a great show, but on the other hand you should not be cutting corners. Remember to keep a miscellaneous budget, for those unseen extras.

RISK ASSESSMENT AND HEALTH & SAFETY

Your show is most likely going to be open to the public, so it is important to consider any risks that might be involved with both the installation and the show itself. If there are any risks, these should be minimised by safe practice.

POSSIBLE RISKS INVOLVED

- Is the object heavy? Are there manual handling considerations?
- Does it involve electricity? (The electricity supply in the UK and Europe is 240v, which is potentially lethal.)
- Are there sharp edges?
- Is the work fragile?
- Could it cause visual/aural disturbance? (e.g. strobe lighting)
- Are there trip hazards?

WHO IS AT RISK?

- Yourself?
- Others (fellow exhibitors, staff, students)?
- The public?
- Consideration should be taken for women who are pregnant, or of child-bearing age, as some substances can be harmful to the unborn child.

WHAT IS THE LEVEL OF RISK?

Consider the worst possible outcome

- Death
- Serious injury
- Minor injury

Think of the actions you might take to make things safer and apply as needed. If there is still a doubt about the safety of the intended work then you may have to rethink. Seek advice as necessary.

ACCESS

Respect all fire corridors and exits, making sure not to obstruct them, as fires can happen at any time. Also, don't obscure fire-exit signs or move fire extinguishers. Legally, the venue has to have them, so they are not negotiable.

LADDERS

If you are working from ladders or at height, never work alone. Check the condition of the ladders and take care when moving them around the space. There may be restrictions on the use of ladders, e.g. in using them over a certain height. These should always be respected, as they are there for a reason. If you have to wait for a ladder, then wait; under no circumstances should you compromise your safety.

INSURANCE

There are different types of insurance to cover different needs, depending upon your status within the organisation or venue you are showing in. It's worth checking out where you stand. You don't want to be sued by someone because your work has fallen off the wall and squashed them, not that it should now you have purchased this guide!

PUBLIC LIABILITY

This covers you if you are sued by a member of the public for causing accidental property damage or injury. If you are a student or member of staff your employer should have this cover in hand. If you are not covered, it is relatively cheap. Short-term cover can be purchased; in this regard, it is best to look for events insurance, which will give cover for a specific event and time frame.

EQUIPMENT

Portable equipment insurance should insure against loss, damage or theft to tools, cameras, projectors, etc. Do not assume you are covered, as many institutions only cover for the loss of very large amounts.

2

stage two

basic tools

notes

BASIC TOOLS – the basic installation hanging kit

No matter what sort of work you're installing, at some point or other you will most likely need some tools. Tools should last a long time, so think of them as an investment. It's worth paying more for good-quality tools, as they will do what they are supposed to do better, and be easier and more enjoyable to use.

Do not assume you can borrow tools from other people; it's worth buying your own. Even if you have access to tools, they may well be on loan to someone else at the moment you need to use them.

I've started off with a 'basic list', but your practice will determine the ones you will definitely need. I will cover other tools in different parts of the guide.

THE BASIC LIST:

Tape measure
Screwdriver(s)
Spirit level
Bradawl
Hand drill*
Cordless drill*
Mains-powered drill*
Stanley knife
Saw
Pliers
Hammer
Chisel (old and best)

Also include plenty of pencils, notepaper, a rubber and masking tape.

notes

* If you have a drill you will need a set of drill bits. An HSS metric set 1.5–6.5 mm (imperial set 1/16 th – 1/4in.) should do most things. If you're drilling into brick walls you will need a masonry bit (see drill pages).

CARRYING/STORAGE

You will need something to carry your tools around with; this is very much a matter of choice. There are a number of carrying systems on the market, including toolboxes. Canvas/nylon tool bags are worth considering; they are comfortable to carry around, with soft handles and no sharp corners. You may be able to adapt something you already have, but remember that tools are irregular shapes and plastic bags don't work.

Personally, I have never got on with toolboxes; at work I usually use a 'soft' canvas bucket with lots of pockets and a carrying strap, into which I can put what I need for a particular task. It tends to have a lot of stuff gathering at the bottom, but this is actually quite useful as I often discover things that are needed for a particular job, but were not planned for. If you're on a tight budget, use a builder's bucket.

Tool belts are really practical, particularly if you are going to be working off ladders. If you have a cordless drill, get a holster for it rather than trying to balance it at the top of a stepladder. Remember that belts should not be worn when installing paintings or other fragile art works.

It's always worth marking your tools, as others will invariably try and borrow them. I am usually pretty mean when it comes to lending things out; they often don't come back when you need them, or worse still they don't come back at all – so take note!

TAPE MEASURE

A 'must have' item. A student once asked to borrow my tape and when I replied in the negative and suggested he buy one, he retorted that he was a film-maker. My response was, "Why ask then?", because, no matter what your practice, you will at some point need a tape measure.

Steel tapes are very accurate and should last a long time, you can buy them with the graduations in either metric on its own or metric and imperial (feet and inches). 13 and 19 mm wide (½ and ¾ in.) blades are the most common; the wider ones are more robust and will remain stiffer when measuring across spaces.

Don't leave them lying about with the blade out; if they get trodden on you will need to buy another one.

Recommended makes:
Fisco
Lufkin
Stanley
Stabila

SCREWDRIVERS

You will probably need at least two screwdrivers, as screws come in a variety of sizes and forms. I would recommend having at least a Pozidriv 2 and a medium-size slotted

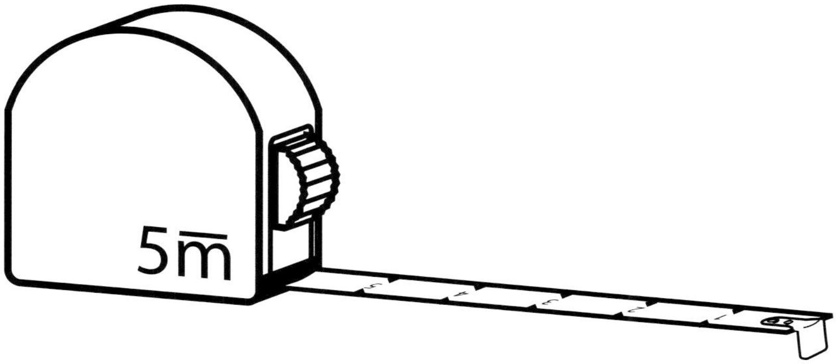

Tape measure

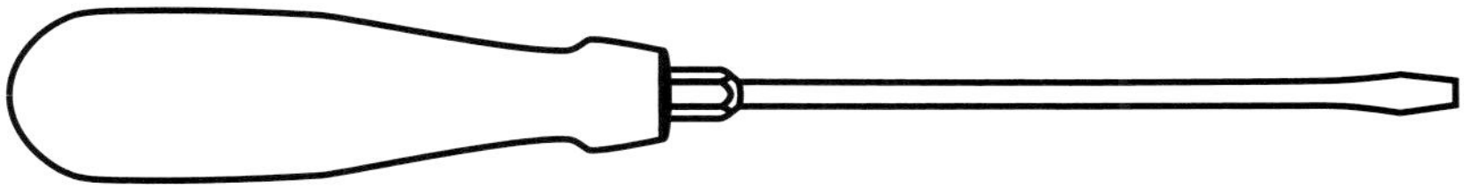

Screwdriver

screwdriver, but you could quite realistically need more than these. For small screws you may need a Pozidriv 1 and/or a small slotted screwdriver. Even if you have a cordless drill/driver, you could often find yourself in a situation where it's preferable or easier to use an ordinary screwdriver.

Buy screwdrivers with comfortable handles, as these will allow you to exert more torque (twisting force). You can also buy screwdrivers with hardened tips, which will last longer. For tight situations you may need a stubby screwdriver; as the name suggests, they have short shafts and bodies. Also available are ratchet or bit-holder types. An old, large, slotted screwdriver is always useful for those jobs for which ideally you should not use a screwdriver, i.e. opening or stirring cans of paint, etc. If you are doing extensive electrical work, you may need a mains-testing screwdriver.

Recommended makes:
Stanley Dynagrip
Stanley 'Yankee' spiral ratchet
Wera
Wiha

SPIRIT LEVEL

For checking whether things are horizontal or vertical. A short level (250 mm/10 in.) is probably the most practical for hanging two-dimensional work; I particularly like scaffolders' levels. A longer level is better for setting out and for building projects (though you can always tape a short level onto something straight). Remember

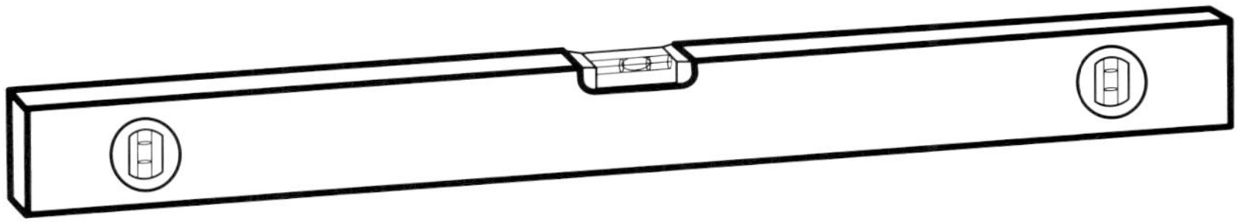

Spirit level

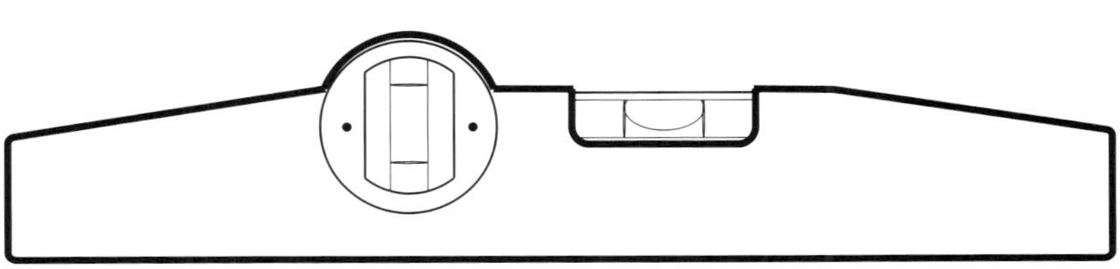

Scaffolder's level

to use the level as a guide, because sometimes, even if accurate, you may need to adjust things by eye, taking into account the fact that walls/floors/corners are often not true. It is not worth buying a cheap level, especially a plastic one!

Recommended makes:
BMI
Stabila
Stanley

BRADAWL

Used for making small holes in wood or board prior to screwing, so as to prevent splitting. These are also good for cleaning out screws (which have been gummed up with filler or paint) if you need to remove them.

Recommended makes:
Crown
Footprint
Irwin Marples
Stanley

HAND DRILL

A bradawl is fine for making small holes in wood, but for anything else you will need some sort of drill. Hand drills are fairly inexpensive; you can buy them with a single or double pinion (drive), the single being cheaper, the double allowing a smoother and more stable operation. Being easy to control, they are good for accurate work – e.g.

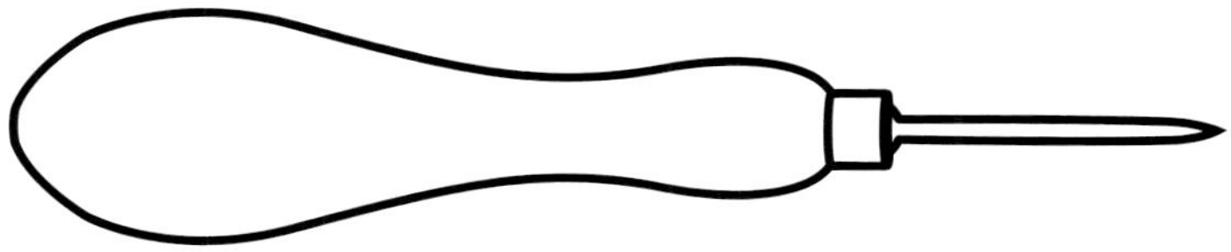

Bradawl

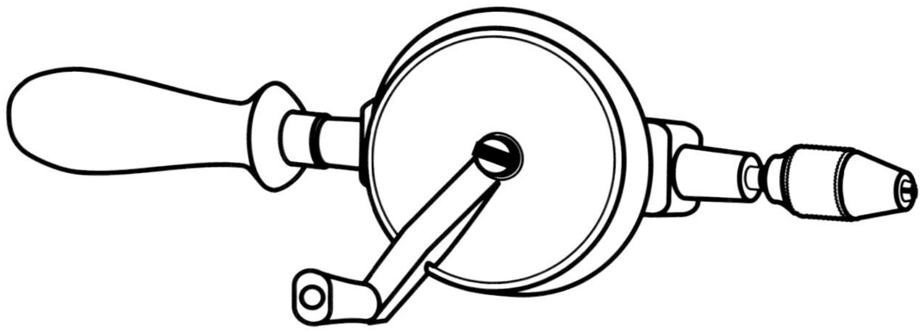

Hand drill

for drilling holes into the back of a frame – and because of their relatively narrow profile they offer greater access in tight situations. They are certainly a better option than a cheap cordless drill. Interestingly, some galleries, including the Tate, will only use hand tools when installing or attaching fixings to art works.

Recommended make:
Stanley

CORDLESS DRILLS

Cordless drills can be roughly divided between DIY and professional models, the latter being more robust, more powerful and better suited to prolonged use (this applies to all power tools). There are two types: combi-drills and drill-drivers. Drill-drivers have the ability to drill holes and to be used as power screwdrivers, whilst combi-drills have the added function of hammer action, i.e. the ability to drill holes into brick or concrete. Unless you are spending a lot on a drill it's probably wise to buy a drill-driver rather than a combi. They also come in a range of voltages – the higher the voltage the greater the power – although the biggest difference is in the working time of the battery. In any case, 12 and 14.4 v are generally more than up to the job, so don't rush out and buy a "bargain" all-singing, all-dancing 18 v mega-monster.

Drills should have a slow and a fast speed, plus forward and reverse, torque control (the amount of turning power), at least two batteries, and a fast charger (full charge within one hour). There is nothing worse than

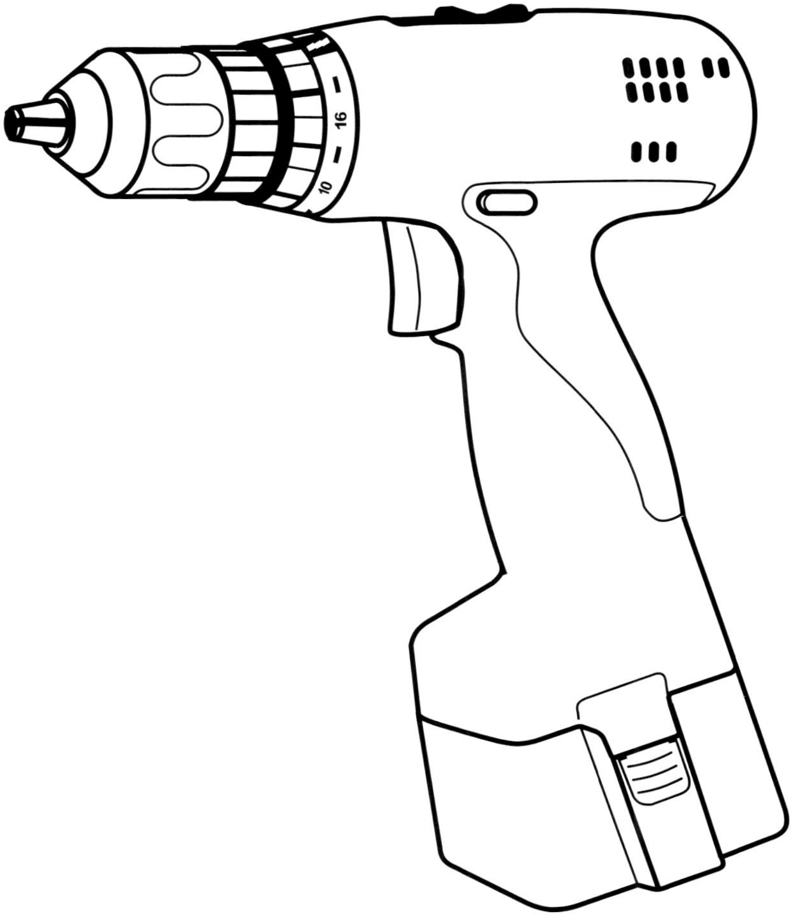

Cordless drill

having to wait for a battery to charge (and they do tend to run down when not in use), so check and recharge before starting work. Remember, drilling into concrete or brick will drain the battery fairly quickly.

Recommended makes:
Bosch
Dewalt
Festool
Hitachi
Makita
Metabo
Black & Decker (DIY)
Ryobi (DIY)

MAINS-POWERED DRILLS

These are usually a more powerful option than a cordless drill, definitely worth considering if you need to do a lot of heavy duty work, i.e. drilling into concrete or brick and fixing items like rawlbolts (see fixings). Again they fall into two categories, DIY and professional. You should buy a mains drill with either hammer action or an SDS type.

Hammer action drills have a standard chuck, which will accept a wide range of bits, with a switch to select hammer function for use with masonry bits. SDS drills have a special chuck and will only accept SDS bits, which have a bayonet fitting. They are extremely efficient, more so than hammer drills. It's worth buying one that has interchangeable chucks i.e. an SDS and standard chuck, so you can also use them with the standard range of bits.

For general use mains drills are not as flexible to use as a cordless, because they have to be plugged in and have trailing leads.

Recommended makes:
Makita
Bosch
Hitachi
Dewalt
Metabo
Black & Decker (DIY)
Ryobi (DIY)

STANLEY KNIFE/CRAFT KNIFE

So called after the manufacturer. An extremely sharp knife with either replaceable or snap-off blades. A variety of different patterns are available. The ones with metal handles and retractable blades are the best bet. The Stanley Titan knives are my particular favourite. Beware of cheap imitations, and remember that the blade should be firmly fixed when cutting.

Recommended makes:
Irwin
Stanley

CLAW HAMMER

Claw hammers are the most versatile hammers. They are made for driving and removing nails, but can also be used for things like tapping in plugs, as well as tapping up or tapping down screws when hanging work. When you buy one, check the balance and weight – it should feel comfortable to hold.

Recommended makes:
Axminster (they sell a good budget hammer)
Estwing
Stanley
Vaughan

SAW

Saws come in a variety of forms to suit different functions or materials. They are classified by type, length of blade, and either teeth per inch or points per inch (TPI or PPI). You're most likely to need a universal handsaw. Most handsaws these days cannot be re-sharpened. They are, however, relatively cheap and should last a reasonable time. I particularly like Bahco's Laminator saw, which has a 51 cm (20 in.) blade and 12 PPI; the blade is thicker and therefore stiffer than most. It's designed for cutting laminate flooring, but is equally good on large timber and boards and because of the stiffness of the blade is good enough for general joinery. If you don't want to carry a long saw you could buy a toolbox saw, which as the name suggests should fit into most toolboxes or bags. Saws should come with a blade guard – hang on to it!

Recommended makes:
Bahco
Irwin
Jack
Stanley

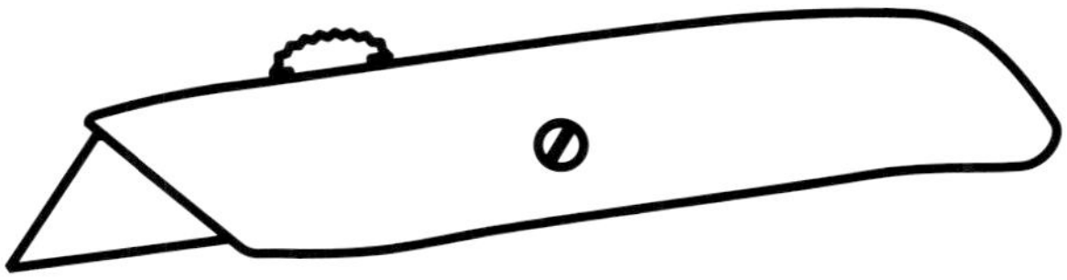

Stanley knife

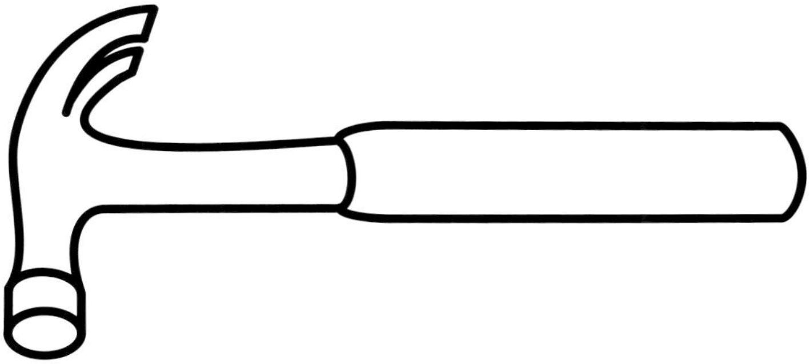

Hammer

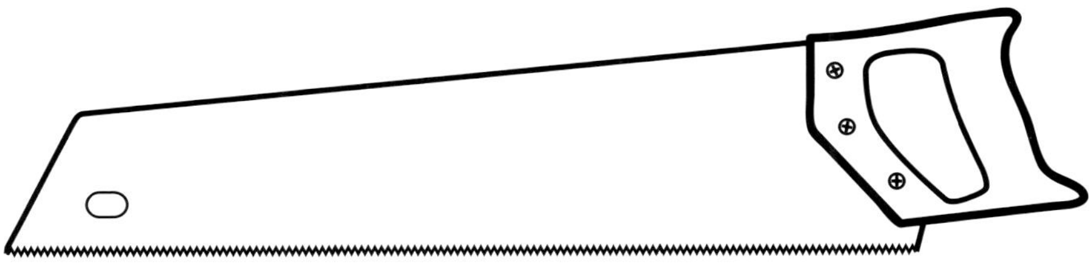

Handsaw

PLIERS

A pair of combination pliers is the most useful, combining the functions of gripping and cutting. They have flat serrated jaws for gripping flat surfaces, and a rounded section for pipes, tubing etc. Behind the gripping section are the cutters. Often included in the main body are wire croppers for cutting thin wire and cable. When buying, check the joint – it should not be stiff, but at the same time it should not be too loose. It is worth buying the ones with comfortable, ergonomic handles. It is also worth considering buying a pair of long-nose pliers, which are good for pulling out staples and other fiddly jobs.

Recommended makes:
Bahco
Knipex
NWS
Stanley

CHISEL

Ideally have two, one kept sharp, the other 'knackered'. Chisels come in a range of sizes and forms, from 3 to 50 mm ($\frac{1}{8}$ – 2 in.) blade width; bevelled-edge chisels are the most common, and a blade either 18 or 25 mm ($\frac{3}{4}$ – 1 in.) wide is a good starting point. Although for any serious joinery work you should use them with a mallet, if you buy one with a plastic, impact-resistant handle you can use it with a hammer, though do wear a glove.

The sharp one should be kept sharp – keep it in the blade guard when not in use – you will find

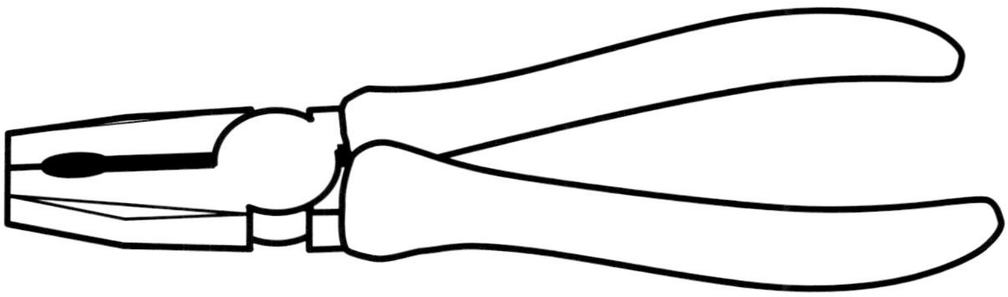

Combination pliers

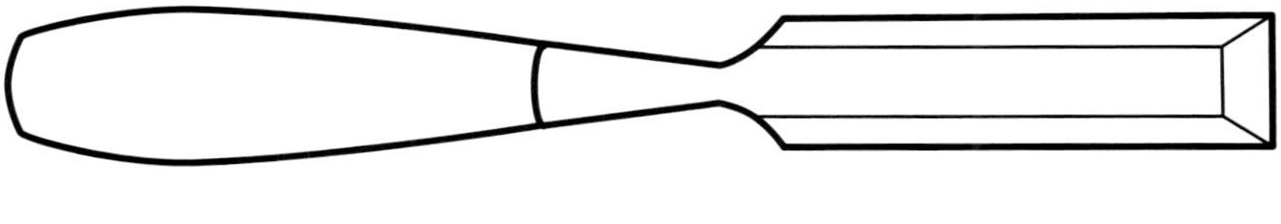

Chisel

it's a useful addition to your toolkit. The 'knackered' one, i.e. the one with a blunt blade, is useful for a variety of jobs such as opening tins, using as a wedge, knocking off bits of filler, etc. Never use the sharp chisel for the above, because the blades are easily chipped.

Recommended makes:
Bahco
Irwin Marples
Stanley

DRILL BITS

HSS BIT

High-speed steel bits are the most commonly used bit, due to their versatility. They can be used to drill wood, metal and plastics, and are available in both metric and imperial sizes. A set of 1.5–6.5 mm in 0.5 mm increments (1/16 – 1/4 in. in 1/32 in. increments) will suffice for most needs – you can always buy larger or in-between-size bits for specific jobs. Do not use for drilling masonry walls.

LIP & SPUR BIT

Similar in appearance to HSS bits, they differ in having a sharp centre point, which means they can be positioned accurately on a marked spot and do not slip. They are particularly useful when drilling into the backs of frames and stretchers, and are for wood use only.

FLAT BIT

For fast drilling of larger holes in wood, between 6 and 38 mm (1/4 – 1 3/4 in.). They are generally 150 mm (6 in.) long and the working length can be increased with an extension shank.

DRILL BITS

HSS bit

Lip & spur bit

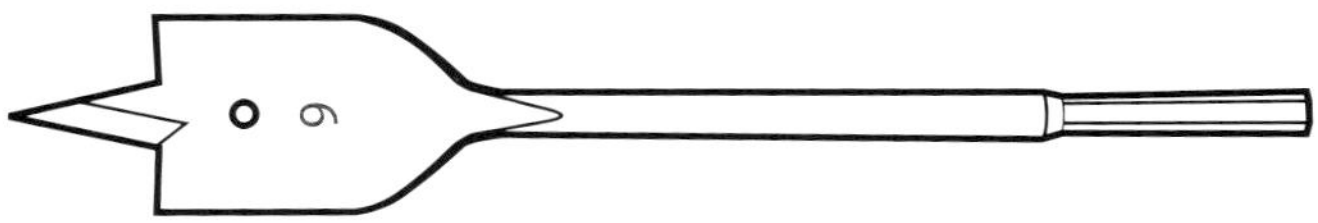

Flat bit

Masonry bit

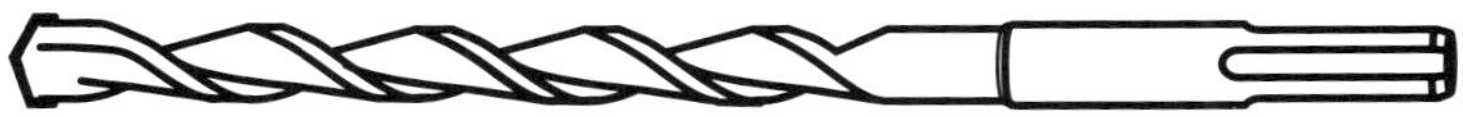

SDS masonry bit

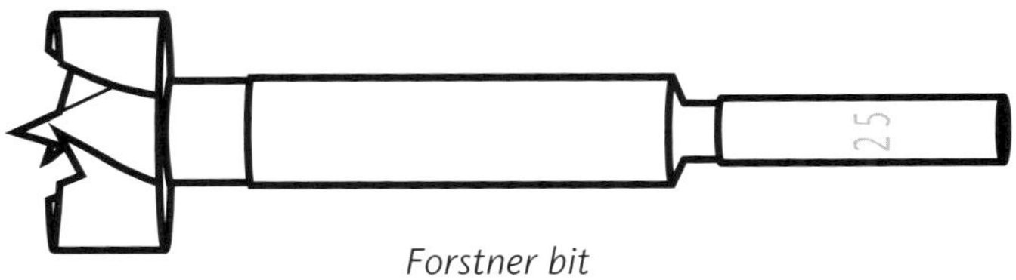

Forstner bit

MASONRY BIT

These drills have a tungsten-carbide tip, which means they are tough enough to drill through stone, brick and concrete. To use properly, you will need a drill with a hammer action.

SDS BIT

These are similar in appearance to masonry bits, with a tungsten-carbide tip. They are made to be used in conjunction with SDS drills, which have a different type of chuck compared with standard drills, hence the grooves in the end of the shank. This combination gives a much more efficient drilling action.

FORSTNER BIT

These bits will give a clean, flat-bottomed cut. They are useful for making recesses in the backs of boards for hanging purposes.

HOLE SAWS

Made for cutting large holes in a wide range of materials. They need to be used in conjunction with an arbor; this is fixed to the drill, the cutter fitted onto it, and it acts as a centring point for the hole. Bosch makes particularly good arbors, which fit all the various sizes from 14 to 152 mm ($^{9}/_{16}$ – 6 in.). They can be used to create ventilation or holes for plugs/leads in plinths, etc.

COUNTERSINKS

These come in various patterns and are used to form a recess when using countersunk screws so that the heads do not protrude. You can also buy combination drill countersinks, which will speed things up. If you don't have one, you can improvise with a large HSS bit.

DRILL BITS & COUNTERSINKS

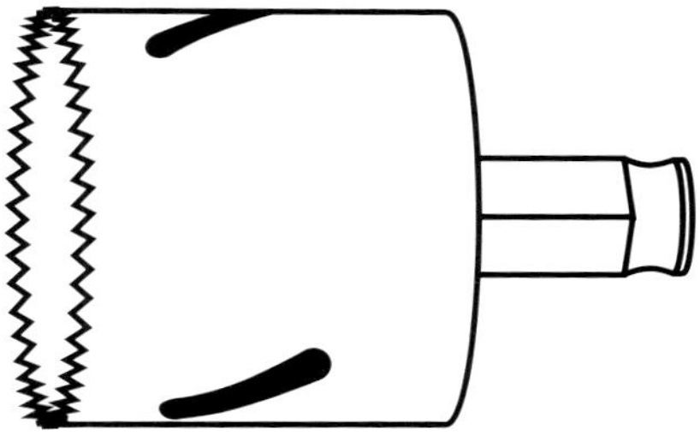

Hole saw

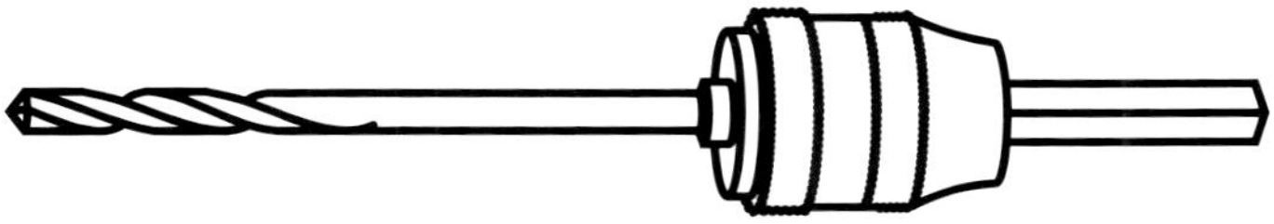

Arbor for hole saw

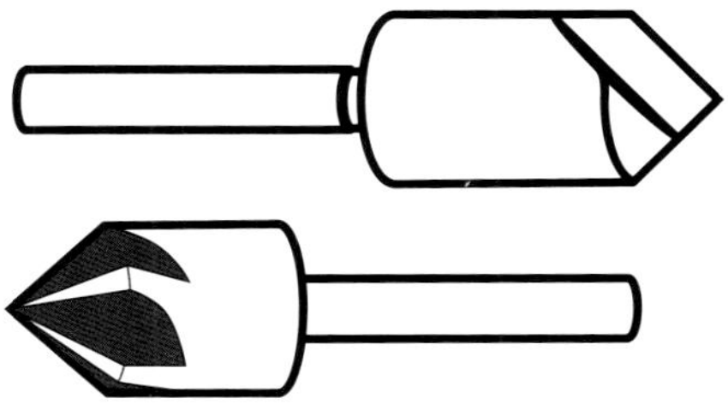

Countersinks

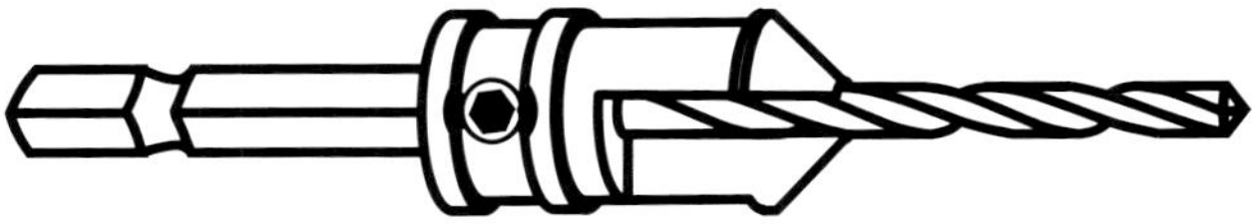

Combination drill/countersink

3

stage three

preparation of space
moving & placing work
packing

PREPARATION OF SPACE

notes

Depending on the venue, you may have to do some preparation or making good of the space. Always talk to the curator or gallery manager (and visit if possible) to see what needs doing, and then allocate time in your schedule accordingly. Most venues will have guidelines as to what you can and cannot do, and some may stipulate what type or colour of paint to use. In some institutions it is usual to leave a deposit if you are going to make changes to the space, e.g. paint the space pink. This would be refunded once you have returned the space to its normal condition within a given time frame.

Remember that whilst the space needs to look good to suit your needs, you are not a painter and decorator. It is very easy to get over absorbed in this task, which then leaves you short of time for the more important bit, installing the work. People will be looking at the work not the quality of the decoration.

EQUIPMENT

Depending on what needs doing, you are going to need some or all of the following:

- **Scraper** These have a broad flat blade that is fairly stiff (or the old chisel – see the previous tools section).

- **Filling knife** Similar to a scraper but with a flexible blade which should be kept clean.

- **Brushes and roller/paint tray**

- **Brown gum tape** For taping gaps between boards. Don't use masking tape; white gum

notes

tape is also available, but the brown works better.

- **Filler** There are lots of different types on the market, but I still think the ones you mix yourself are the best, and they're also easy to sand. Because you can mix up just the quantity you need, you don't run the risk of the rest drying up in the pot. Avoid using two-part fillers, particularly when you're covering screws that may need to be removed at some point.

- **Sandpaper** It is good to use this with a sanding block (an offcut of 50 x 25 mm/2 x 1 in. timber with the edges rounded off will suffice), and you may also wish to wear gloves. Avoid using electrical sanders on walls, as these create large quantities of airborne dust.

- **Newspaper/sheets of cardboard** Use for covering the floor when painting walls. Avoid using plastic sheets for this task, as the paint does not dry quickly on plastic if spilt and you run the risk of treading on wet paint, then spreading it through the building. Don't confuse dust sheets with paint covers; dust sheets are what they say they are and will let paint through.

- **Cleaning materials** Sometimes the space may just require a good clean – it's quicker than painting over dirt! It's also good to have cleaning materials on hand in case of accidents and spillages. A student once managed to drop a bucket of paint over me – I'm still not sure whether it was deliberate or not – so beware!

- Which reminds me – wear old clothes!

notes

GUIDELINES

FILLING

Use as little filler as possible, take off any excess, leave to dry, sand back and then refill if necessary. It's bad practice to cake it on, which only leaves you with a lot of sanding.

BROWN GUM TAPE

Often used in college spaces on temporary walls, to cover gaps between boards and screw holes. Galleries usually prefer a more professional finish, so they use filler. Gum tape can be cut to the length required. I find it best to run it through a bowl of water to make it nice and wet. It's then applied to the wall and the excess water is squeezed out. Use the side of your hand or a sponge/cloth to make it flat; there should not be any ripples at this point. Allow to dry before painting over it. When painted over, it may bubble up a bit, but should flatten out again once the paint is dry; if it doesn't, you will have to start again.

PAINTING

Don't be sloppy. I have seen spaces look worse after painting than before. Use plenty of newspaper to cover the floor, on which to place tins of paint, brushes, rollers and trays. It's better to use two coats of paint, if needed, than one which is painted on like butter. Clean up any spills as you go. The point at which the wall meets the floor should be as neat and straight as possible – it makes a huge difference as to how a space appears. Allow for the drying time of paint, which if oil-based may be as much as eight hours, or even longer if you are painting a floor. Let other people know there is wet paint in the space, mark off and put up signs. Clean up brushes, rollers, etc. immediately. Check your feet before leaving the space to avoid trailing paint where it isn't wanted.

STAINS AND COLOURED WALLS

You may have the misfortune of inheriting a space where there is bleed-through from previous use. Emulsion paint won't stop the problem, but oil-based undercoat usually does the trick and once dry this can be painted over with emulsion. Don't use gloss paint. Silver aluminium paint is particularly good for really stubborn stains such as those left from permanent felt-tips or paintballs!

If the walls have been previously painted a bright or dark colour, use a base paint to start with, such as Dulux Trade Problem Solving Basecoat, Dulux Trade Stain Block Plus or Leyland Super Leytex Emulsion which will save you from applying countless coats of paint.

NB Do not eat or drink in the space, but go elsewhere when you want to have a break.

MAKING GOOD

Unless otherwise agreed it is usually your responsibility to make good the space once the show has finished. This means you should remove all your work, fittings, screws, etc., and make good, i.e. fill any holes you have made. If you've altered the space, put it back as agreed. It's very easy to cop out at this point; don't. Be professional about it and remember it's a small world – word gets round!

MOVING AND PLACING WORK

OK, you've got the space – now you need to put the work in it! Here are some basic rules:

- Move the work as little as possible.
- If you have to prepare the space with the work in it, make sure it's covered and protected so as not to get in the way or be damaged.
- When drilling holes, etc., make sure the work is out of the way.
- Consider manual handling (see below).
- Place all the work in the space before you hang anything. Allow lots of time for this task. If the pieces are wall items you can place them around the room. If the work is particularly delicate, it might be good practice to use decoys, i.e. photocopies of the original.
- Do you need to wear gloves? If you do, make sure you can carry the object without it slipping.
- Strips of foam are useful for placing items on, particularly for delicate or framed/glazed work.

MANUAL HANDLING (BASICS)

Stop and think. Plan the lift and assess the weight. Do you need help or lifting/moving aids? Where is the load going? Move any obstructions or trip hazards before you start. For long lifts, consider resting points.

Wear comfortable clothes, not too tight, and suitable shoes. For some items – e.g. boards, heavy objects and materials – it is wise to wear a pair of boots or shoes with steel toecaps. It is also worth using gloves, to avoid splinters and to offer a firmer grip. I particularly like gripper gloves; these are knitted cotton with a latticework of latex, offering excellent grip. Some delicate works, such as photographic or three-dimensional works that have a sensitive surface, may need handling with white cotton gloves. If so, check that you are able to carry the object without losing your grip.

Keep the load close to the waist, as close as possible to the body and with the heaviest side of the load next to the body. Two basic methods of lifting are taught: the leg lift and the semi-squat (see diagram).

Adopt a stable position. Place your feet at an angle to each other, in the case of the leg lift slightly more than shoulder width apart; in the case of the semi-squat lift, the feet should be slightly further apart than hip width.

Get a firm grip. Make sure you can hold the load comfortably, pulling it towards your body if possible.

Adopt a good posture. Bending your knees and keeping your back straight, use your leg and bum muscles to do the work, not your back.

Avoid twisting and leaning sideways. Shoulders should be level and facing the same direction as the hips. Do not lift and twist at the same time.

Keep the head up when handling. Look ahead and not down. Once the load is being held securely, move smoothly without jerking.

MANUAL HANDLING

Moving aids

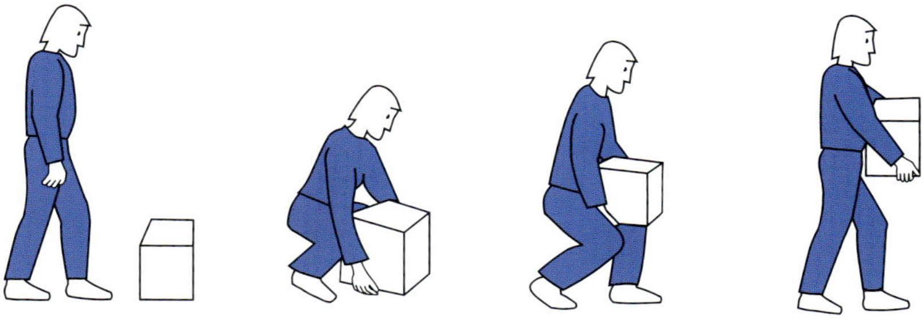

Leg lift

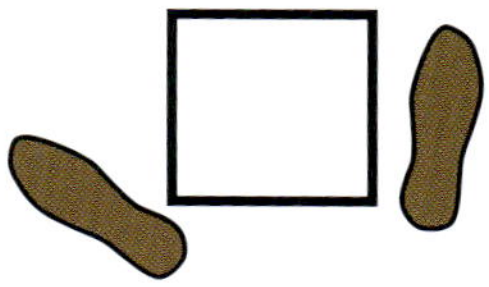

Feet position for leg lift

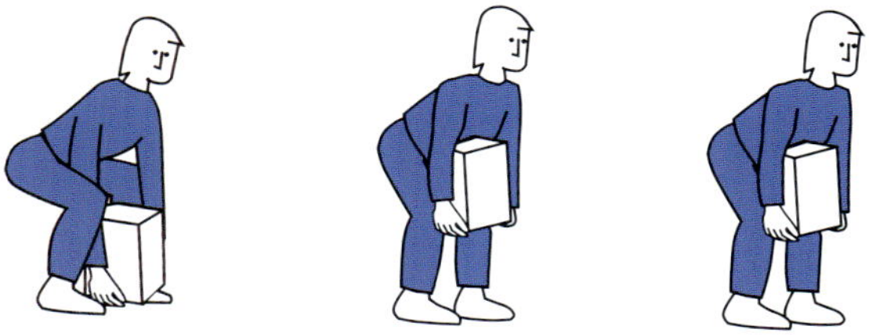

Squat lift

Do not lift more than you can easily manage. There is a difference between what a person can lift and what they can safely lift. The load-limit diagram gives some average male and female lifting capabilities.

NB Most weight can be carried near the body at lower-waist height, with your arms hanging down, hence the term: 'knuckle height'.

Put down the same way: bending the knees, back straight, load close to the body.

MOVING LARGER ITEMS

Larger items may need more than one person to move them, so it's important to decide before lifting who is going to take the lead, and give clear, precise instructions. Preferably, the team should consist of people of similar size and ability, so that the load is evenly distributed.

It is easier to carry boards between two, but make sure the board is leaning in the same direction for both the front and back person (see diagram).

Paintings on canvas/stretchers should be handled with care, making sure that your knuckles do not dig into the back of the canvas; again, two people should be used to carry larger works.

You may find you need straps, or even a skate, to help lift some items. Teflon strips can also be used to slide items across the floor.

LOAD LIMITS

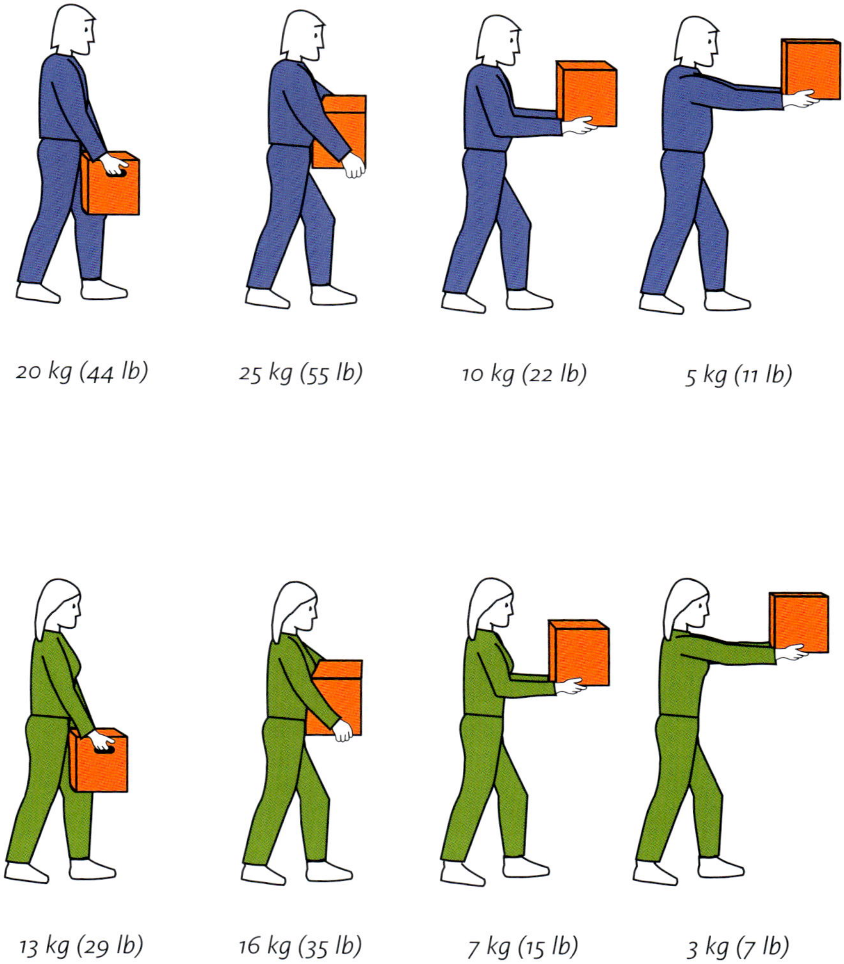

20 kg (44 lb)
25 kg (55 lb)
10 kg (22 lb)
5 kg (11 lb)
13 kg (29 lb)
16 kg (35 lb)
7 kg (15 lb)
3 kg (7 lb)

PACKING

Moving work from one place to another can result in it being damaged. To avoid this you will need to think about packing. The sort of packing required is going to depend on several things: the type of work, how easy the art work is to move, the form of transportation, and who is doing the moving. So it could entail anything from simply protecting the corners of flat 2D work, to constructing purpose-made packing cases if the item is to be shipped.

BASICS

2-DIMENSIONAL WORK

If the surface of the painting, print or photograph is delicate, cover it with acid-free tissue before wrapping it with a clear polythene sheet. The corners can then be added, i.e. either stapled or taped with packing tape, to the back of the frame. Bubble wrap is ideal for wrapping work, but make sure the bubble side is folded in on itself, so that the bubbles don't make direct contact with the work (see fig. 1). This is then folded around the corners (figs 2, 3 and 4). Keep hold of the corners, even when the work has been unwrapped, as the work can stand on them whilst waiting to be hung. You will also need the packing for the return journey.

If the work is going in the back of a van, make sure everything is tied in and secure. Stack properly, with the largest works going in first. Avoid one item digging into another. Blankets are used to separate one work from another within a stack. Smaller works can be stacked in cardboard boxes (with additional packing material between them as necessary). Make sure they are secure.

MOVING BOARDS

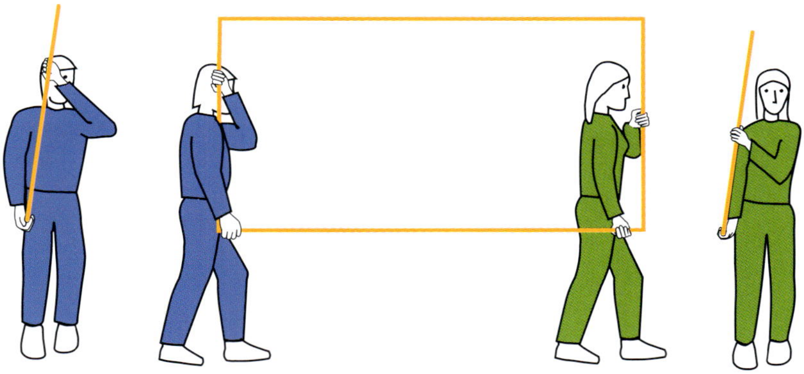

3-DIMENSIONAL WORK

If the work has a delicate surface, cover it with acid-free tissue, before wrapping it with bubble wrap. Once again, fold the bubble wrap in on itself, as this will give you a double layer and keeps the bubble surface off the objects. If necessary, add extra layers to sharp corners. Do this as neatly as possible, making sure the object is still movable. For larger items you may need to add handles as necessary. Small works can be boxed. Large items may need to be put on a pallet if going in a van. Remember to make sure everything is secure; you don't want heavy items shifting around in the back of a van or car. Lengths of flat webbing make useful ties, securing straps and handles.

MARKING

Make sure all wrapped works are clearly marked with the words FRAGILE, HANDLE WITH CARE, and with TOP and direction arrows showing the right way up.

PACKING CASES

Simple packing cases are not too difficult to construct. It may be wise to consider this option, particularly if the work is large and/or delicate. If the work is being freighted by plane or over long distances, it's essential. If your budget allows, get your work packed and crated professionally.

MAKING A BASIC PACKING CASE

Crates are made from plywood and softwood battens. Ply is used because of the way it is made – it withstands impacts and is less likely to hole. Do not use MDF or hardboard. Use exterior ply, preferably 9 mm (3/8 in.), although

CORNERS

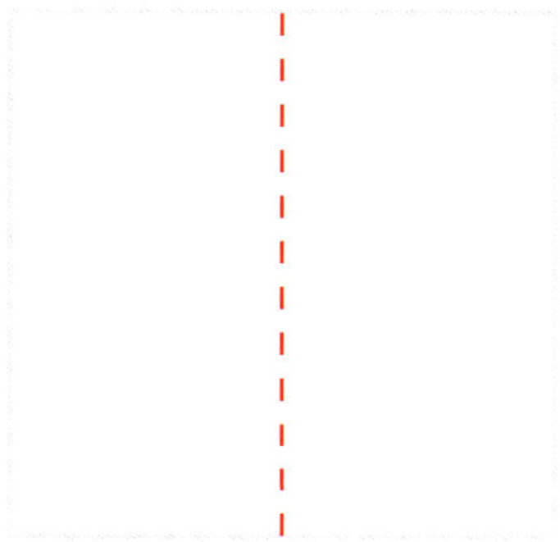

fig. 1

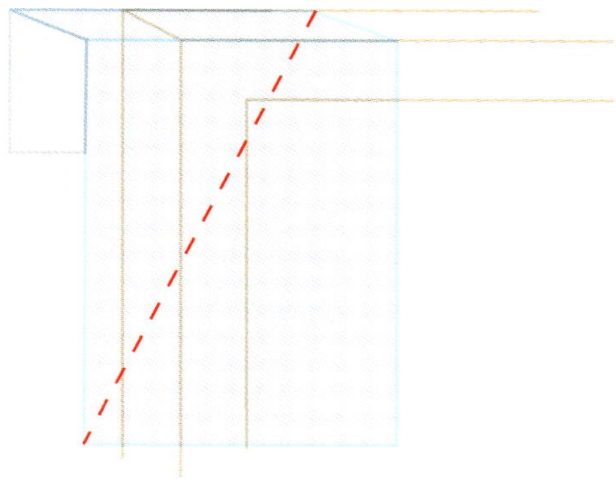

fig. 2

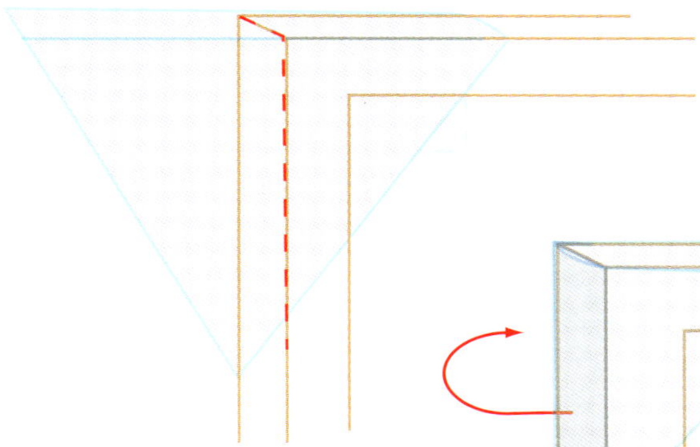

fig. 3

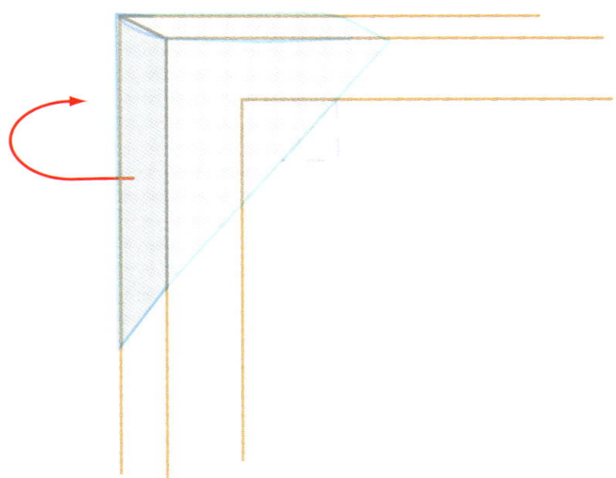

fig. 4

6 mm (¼ in.) will do for less hazardous journeys. For large items and greater strength, 9 mm (⅜ in.) ply is used for the sides and 18 mm (¾ in.) for top and bottom. The battens can be 25 x 50 mm (1 x 2 in.) or larger, i.e. 25 x 75 mm (1 x 3 in.) or even 25 x 100 mm (1 x 4 in.), for greater strength.

Size matters

Make the crate big enough for both the work and any additional packing, i.e. bubble wrap (as above) plus high-density foam if required.

Decide which way the case is to be opened; the usual way is from the top, although 3-dimensional items may require a side opening for ease of handling. Whichever is the opening, remember not to glue it.

Next proceed as follows:

- Cut the ply to size, taking into account overlaps and the addition of the softwood battens (fig. 1).

- Cut the softwood battening, making the vertical lengths run from top to bottom and inserting the horizontal pieces. Glue and screw these into place from the ply through to the softwood, making sure that the screws are properly sunk (fig. 2).

- Add the cross battens to the top and bottom pieces (fig. 3).

- Assemble the sides as in fig. 4 for a top-opening crate, using glue and screws, then add the bottom. For side-opening crates, make sure the opening side sits on the outside (fig. 5).

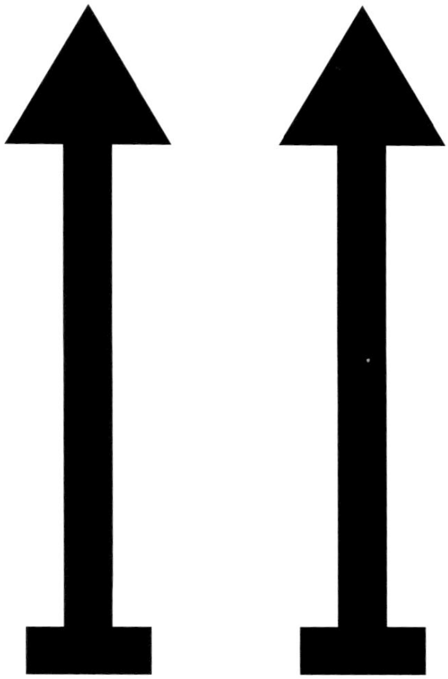

FRAGILE

- Cut the softwood handles to size and glue and screw into place. You may wish to round off the bottom edges for a more comfortable lift.

- Finally, loosely screw on the top without glue. It's not a bad idea to mark round these removable screws with a circle to denote their function. Add arrows and other signage. It may not always be wise to specify the contents.

For further advice on construction, see the Making Plinths section.

MAKING CRATES notes

fig. 1

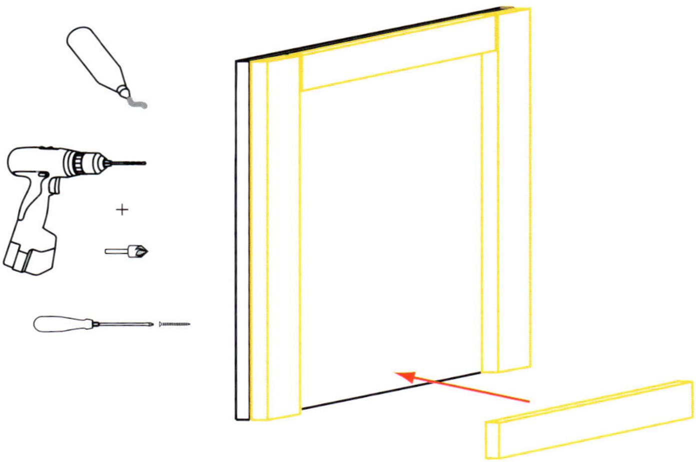

fig. 2

MAKING CRATES

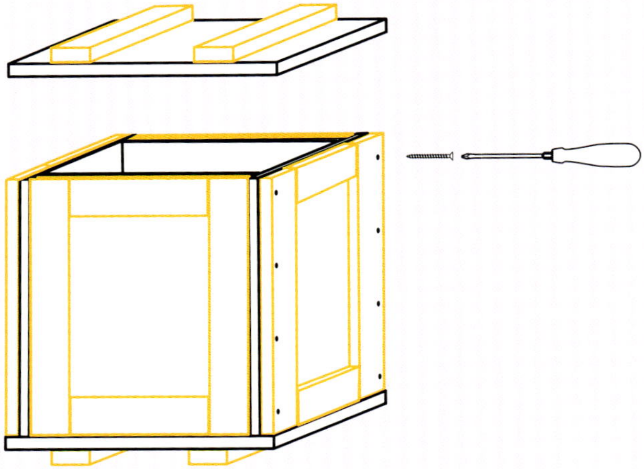

fig. 3

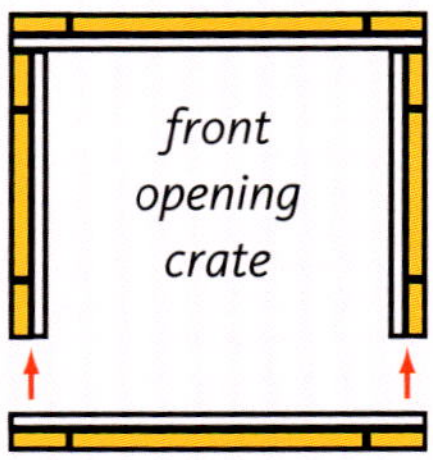

fig. 4

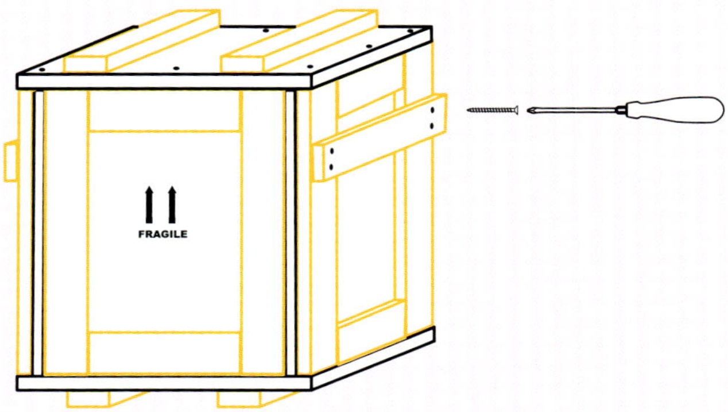

fig. 5

4

stage four

fixings

notes

FIXINGS

If it's work that needs hanging or attaching, what sort of fixing do you want to use? There are several things to consider: what type of structure you are fixing into; what load the work exerts; whether it will be safe; and finally any aesthetic considerations.

LOADING AND FORCES

Think of the weight of the work you're installing. If it's wall-based, is it fairly flat or does it project from the wall? For example, an oil painting, painted on canvas and supported by a stretcher, is essentially a flat object. When it is hung on the wall, most of the weight is straight down and there is minimal force pulling it away from the wall. If it's hung on the wall supported by screws, unless the screws shear it is unlikely to fall off. As long as the screws are properly fixed this is highly unlikely, as screws will hold an enormous vertical weight (fig.1).

However, if the object sticks out from the wall – let's say like a CRT monitor on a shelf or bracket – there is considerable outward as well as downward force, and unless properly fixed it will undoubtedly detach itself from the wall (fig. 2). Think of holding a heavy bag next to and away from your body, and the difference in the force exerted. It's going to take a stronger fixing to hold the monitor than the painting.

If you're hanging anything from the ceiling, all the load is pulling down, so if the fixing is less than completely secure the weight of the object will pull it out (fig. 3).

FORCES

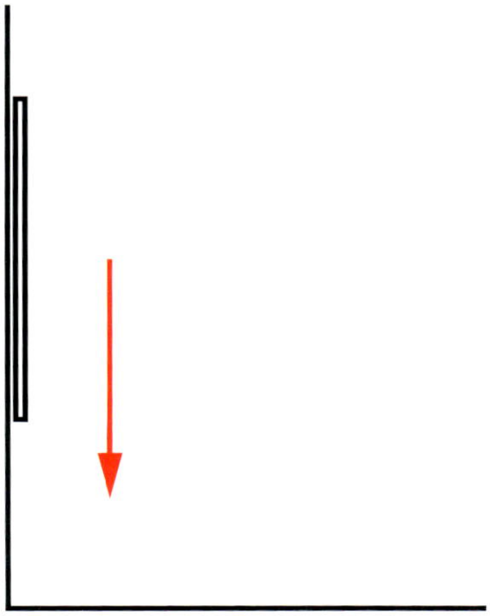

fig. 1

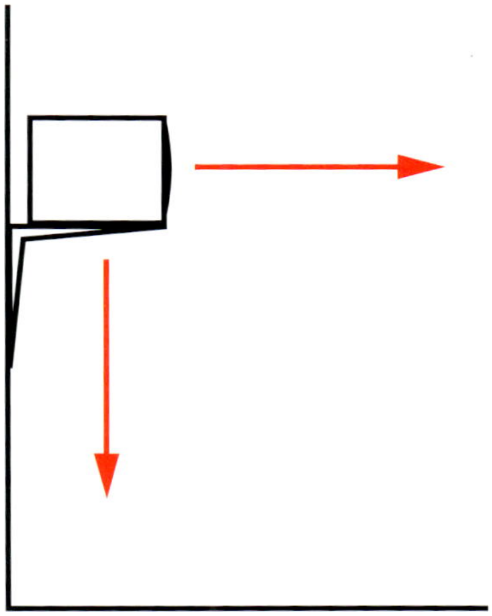

fig. 2

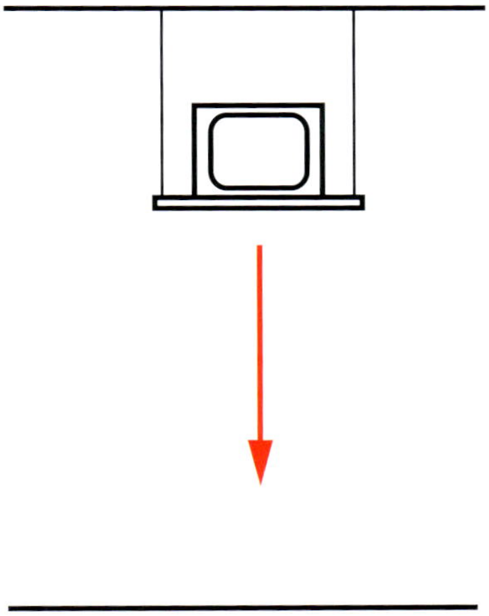

fig. 3

SECURE FIXING INTO WALLS, CEILINGS OR FLOORS

You are likely to come across walls and surfaces made of wood, plaster, brick, etc., and each will need a different approach.

WALLS

Wooden board

It's fairly common for gallery/studio spaces to have the walls lined with wooden board, usually chipboard or ply, or even, sadly, MDF. These are easier to use and are relatively cheap to renovate, and they allow change to be made to the space as needed. The boards are usually attached to a timber frame, which means there will be a small cavity (gap) between the original structural wall and the boards.

Plasterboard

You will also come across spaces that have been lined with plasterboard. As the name suggests, these boards are basically a sheet of plaster in a thin paper sandwich. The plasterboard may then have been skimmed over with a thin layer of plaster to give it a smooth homogeneous look. Most modern domestic interior walls are made this way; the board is attached to either a timber or metal framework (studding). Ceilings are also commonly finished in the same way, with the plasterboard being attached to the underside of the floor joists.

Brick/Masonry

If the space is a shell or is bare, then it has most likely been constructed with brick or sometimes concrete. If the building is relatively modern then building/breeze blocks are the more likely material. These come in two varieties: light- weight ones, which have a lot of ash in them, or concrete. They are much

SCREWHEADS

Pozidriv

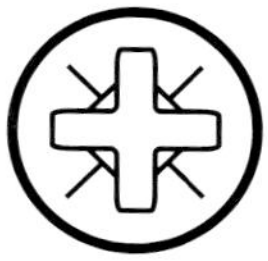

Slotted

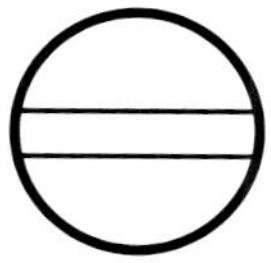

Phillips

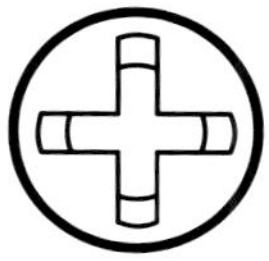

SupaDriv

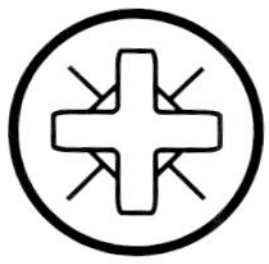

Torx

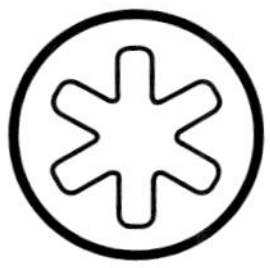

Hexagonal (Allen)

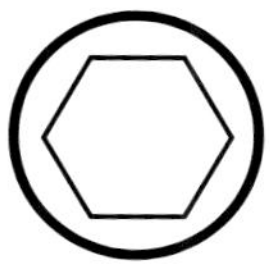

Snake eye

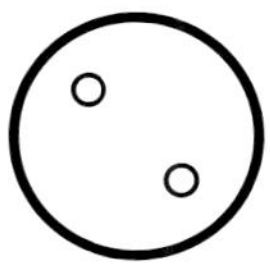

larger than bricks and thus offer a faster and cheaper method of wall building.

Some spaces are completely unfinished so you will see the brickwork, etc.; in others the surface will have been plastered or rendered.

CEILINGS

Apart from plasterboard, you will encounter either bare or suspended/floating ceilings. Bare ceilings are most likely to be concrete, or occasionally the undersides of floorboards and joists.

Suspended ceilings are false ceilings which float away from the shell. They can be quite flimsy, constructed from lightweight panels on a metal framework; so if you're intending to hang anything heavy, you might find it necessary either to go back to the shell or to construct a hanging device.

It is imperative to seek both advice and permission from whoever is in charge of the space before hanging anything from the ceiling. Ceilings may be ornate and/or intrinsically fragile. They may also conceal a minefield of hidden plumbing and electrics.

Hanging anything from existing fittings – e.g. lighting tracks or electrical conduits – could be dangerous and should be avoided.

FLOORS

As with ceilings, there are often restrictions on making holes in floors, as these can be difficult to make good. It's a good idea to talk to the gallery or building manager about any plans to disturb the surface.

Again, there are a variety of types to consider:

SCREW TYPES

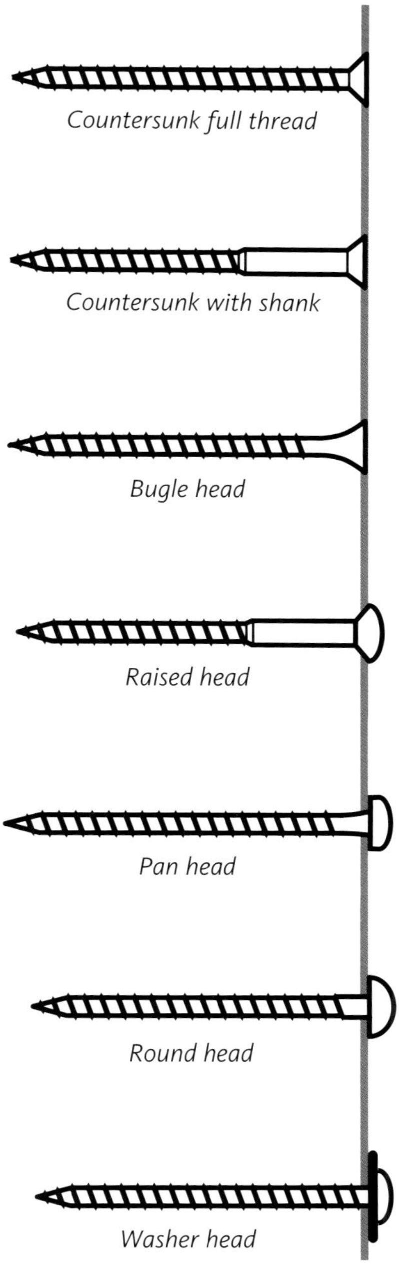
Countersunk full thread
Countersunk with shank
Bugle head
Raised head
Pan head
Round head
Washer head

Wooden floors

These may be floorboards (planks) or made from sheet wood, such as ply or chipboard (this will be flooring grade to withstand the greater wear). Boards or planks may be either attached to joists or sitting on a solid floor. Concrete or composite floors may be bare or painted and, if fixing is possible, can be treated in the same way as masonry walls.

Coverings

Linoleum or vinyl are quite common; these are stuck to the levelled surface.

Carpet tiles are also fairly common but not always suitable for placing work directly onto. Sometimes, you will have to work around a space. For example, I once made a floor-based work for the Natural History Museum in London, and the floor was carpet-tiled. In the end, for both aesthetic and safety reasons I made some huge, low plinths for the work to sit on.

Electricity If the cable is not surface-mounted, never drill or fix vertically above or below any socket or switch as you run the risk of going through a live cable. This can be fatal.

OTHER SCREW TYPES

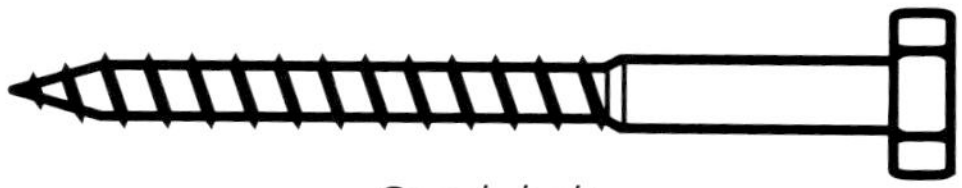

Coach bolt

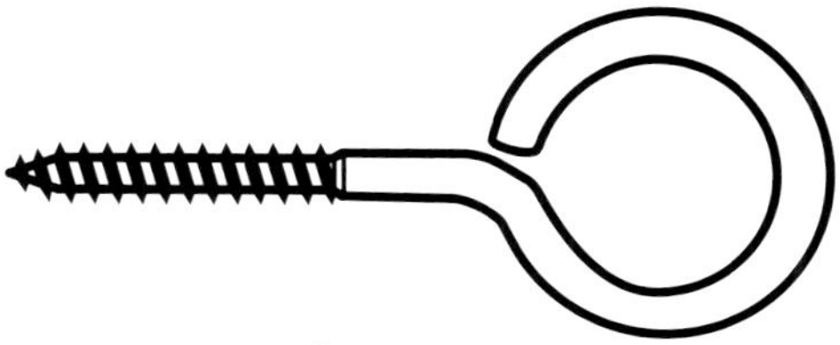

Screw eye

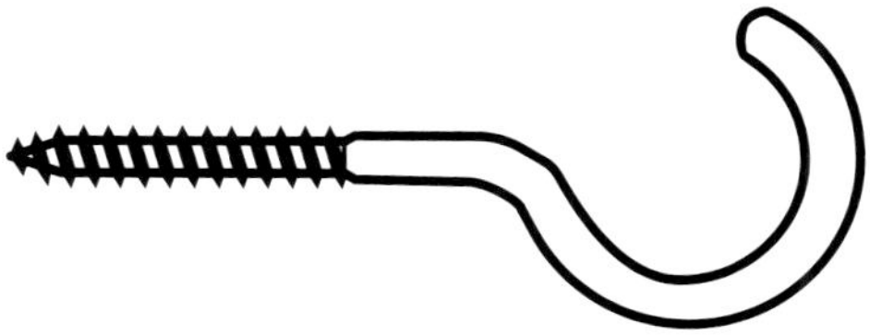

Screw hook

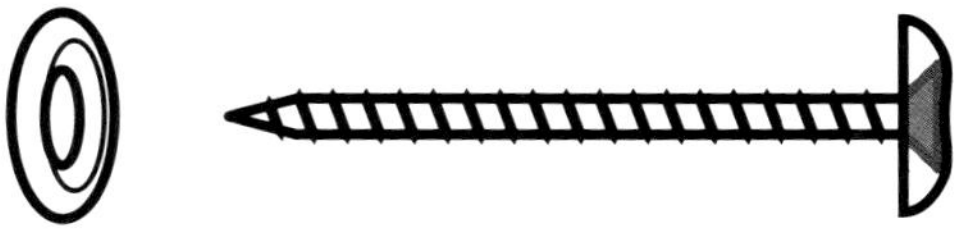

Countersunk screw with screw cup

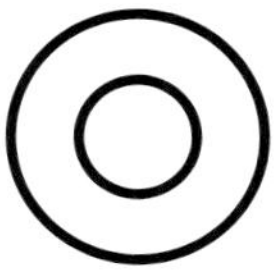

Washer

TYPES OF FIXING

RAWLPLUGS™ (PLASTIC WALL PLUGS)

Rawlplug™ has become a generic name, deriving from the name of the manufacturer Rawl Fixings, for the common plastic wall plugs used for fixing into masonry walls, etc. They come in various sizes and are usually colour-coded (see the size guide below), brown and red being the most commonly used. You will come across various brands on the market – e.g. Fischer, Rawl, Plasplug – but they are all essentially the same. Some have 'wings', some don't; but they will all do the same job.

Size guide – in metric (imperial)

Colour	Screw range	Bit size
Yellow	3.0–4.0 (4–8)	5 (13/64 in.)
Red	3.5–5.0 (6–10)	6 (15/64 in.)
Brown	4.0–6.0 (8–12)	7 (17/64 in.)
Blue	4.5–6.0 (9–12)	8 (5/16 in.)
Grey	5.0–8.0 (10–18)	10 (25/64 in.)

Rawlplugs™ are suitable for small and medium loads – for example, paintings, framed drawings, battening, shelves, etc.

If you're fixing something to a wall, offer the piece up, position and mark through with a sharp pencil. Alternatively, if the piece is too thick, pre-drill the hole and mark with the standard drill bit, or put a nail through the hole and tap through with a hammer to mark the wall. Drill the hole with a masonry or SDS bit that is the correct size for the selected plug. Push the plug into the hole with your thumb, then tap it in with a hammer. It should be a snug fit; if too loose it will not hold

RAWLPLUGS™ (WALL PLUGS)

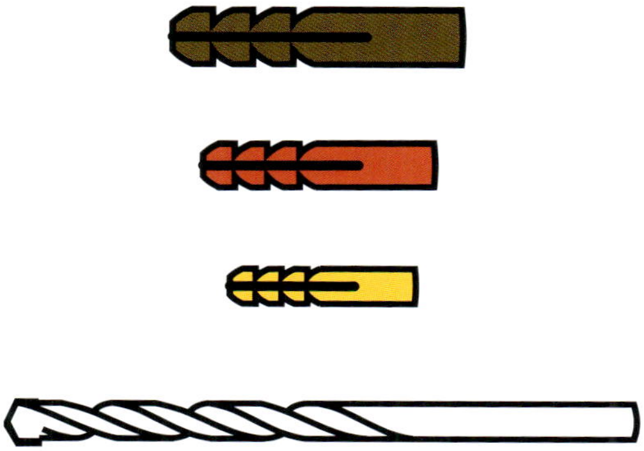

Use masonry bit

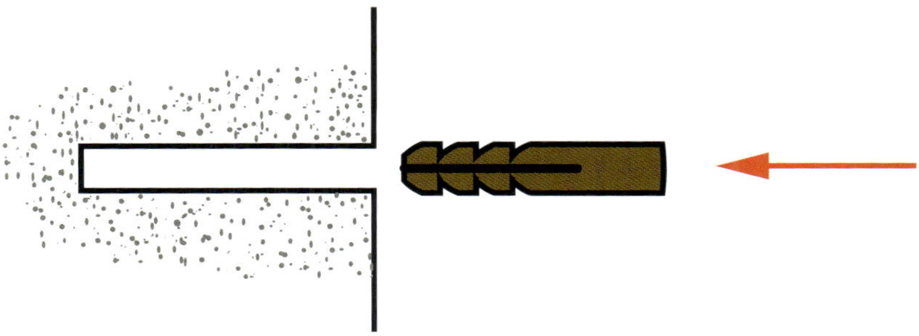

fig. 1

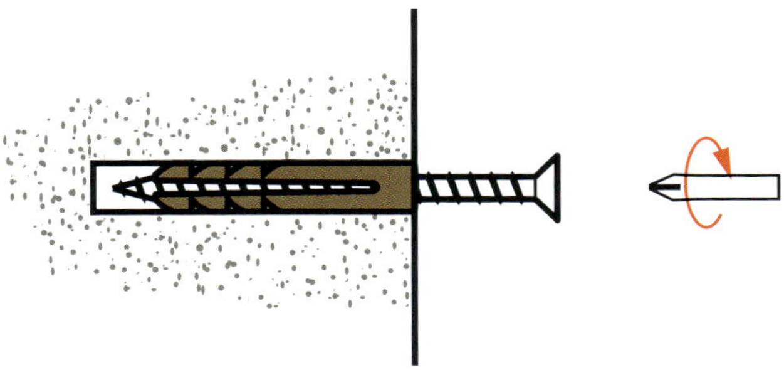

fig. 2

properly, if too tight the plug will snap before it's properly in the hole. The item can then be screwed in.

If you're hanging something like a large painting, which needs to be level but has more than one fixing, it's often a good idea to fix one side first. Offer up the painting and position it, mark the wall on one side, drill and fix. It's then easier to level the painting when marking and fixing the other side (see Hanging 2-dimensional work, page 77).

TIPS: When drilling into walls, tape or hold a small box, envelope or folded stiff paper, underneath the hole to catch the dust.

If you need to put very thin screws or pins into the wall, use bits of matchstick or slivers of wood to fill the centre hole of the plug, or just drill a small hole and jam it with matchsticks/slivers (this is how fixings were made before the invention of Rawlplugs™). A box of matches is a useful addition to your toolbox.

OTHER TYPES OF FIXING

Various fixings have evolved from the basic Rawlplug™ for particular uses, e.g. plastic fixings for plasterboard and thin sheeting used to make cavity walls. There are also a number of 'universal' fixings on the market such as Rawl's UNO and Fischer's Universal UX, which their respective manufacturers claim are suitable for all types of wall.

However, if the horizontal or vertical load is too great there can be a danger of fixings pulling

PLASTERBOARD FIXING

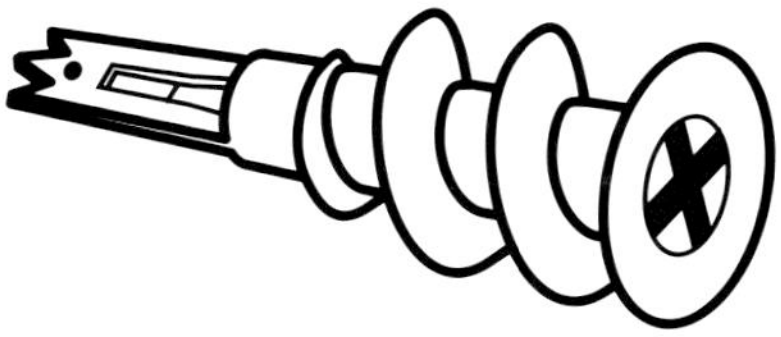

plus

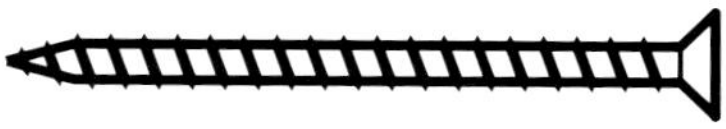

or

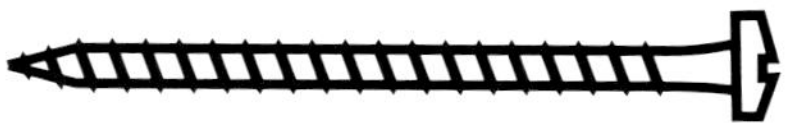

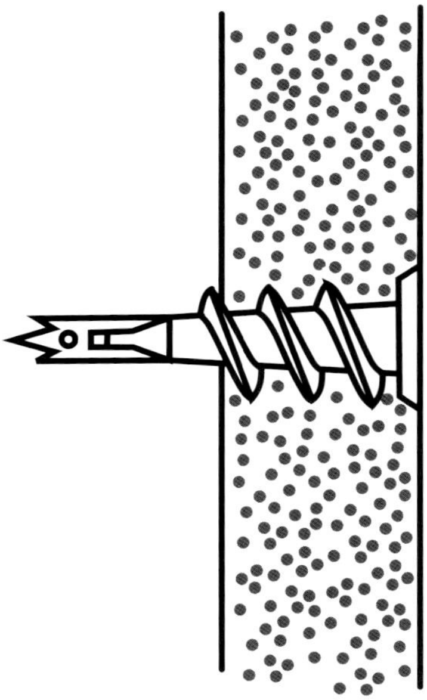

fig. 1

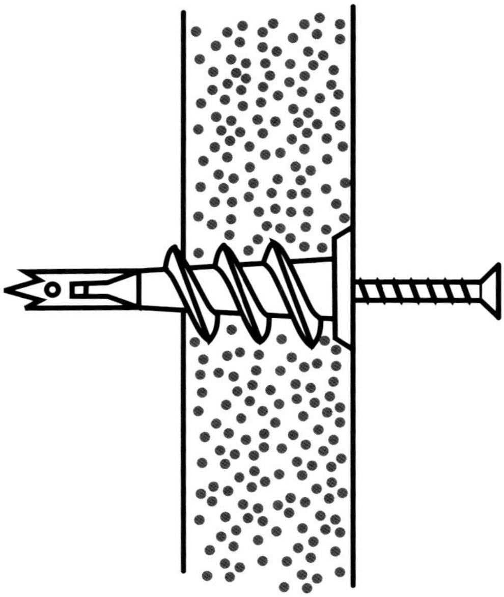

fig. 2

out, so you may have to consider other types.

PLASTERBOARD FIXINGS

Plasterboard is basically a plaster sandwich between two layers of paper and, as you can imagine, it will not take much of a load. Screws will pull straight out, and only light loads can be hung using the plastic Rawl-type fixings.

Plasterboard fixings can be used for light-medium loads; I use the metal rather than the plastic versions. They can be purchased with screws, usually pan-headed or washer (see Screw types, page 59), but can be used with any wood or board screw with a gauge of 4.0–5.0 (8–10), as they will self-tap, i.e. cut their own thread.

The fixing itself is screwed directly into the board (fig. 1). For greater accuracy you can drill a pilot hole. The screw is then screwed into the fixing (fig. 2).

For higher loads consider attaching a plate to spread the weight; consider also, or instead, finding the studding (the structure that the plasterboard is fastened to), which may be either wood or metal. You will find studs where the boards join and hopefully at set points in between. It may mean you have to do some experimental drilling – i.e. drill along a horizontal line until you hit something solid. Alternatively, you could get a stud detector. You can then put screws with confidence through the plasterboard and fix into the studding.

SPRING TOGGLES

These consist of a threaded bolt with a nut that has a pair of folding sprung wings attached (see illustration). They can be used in walls

SPRING TOGGLE

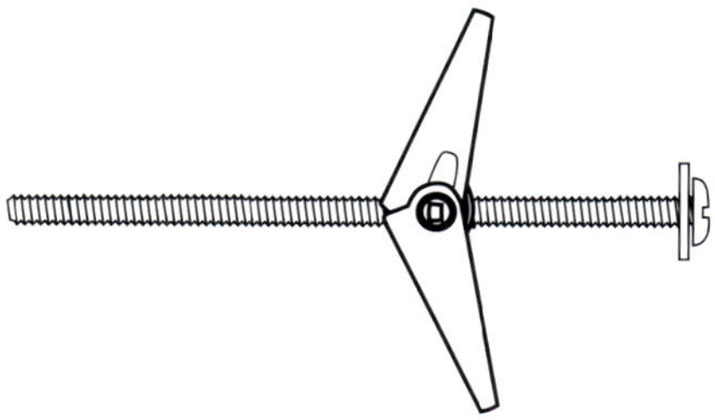

HSS bit or

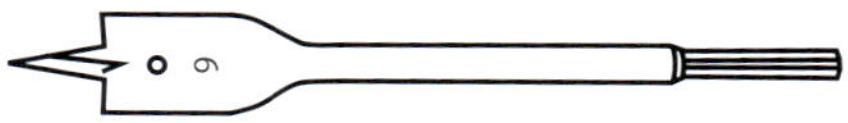

flat bit

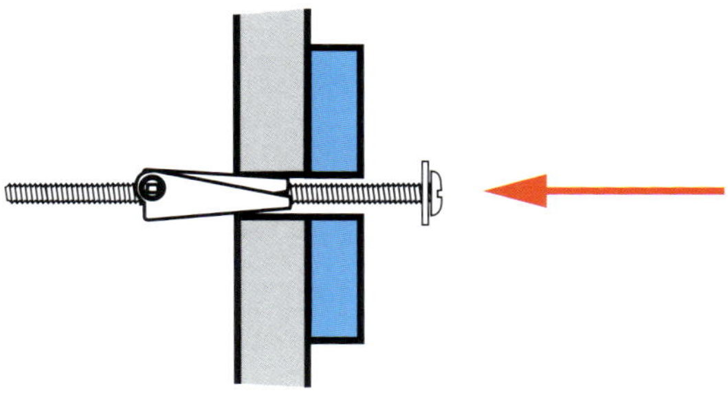

fig. 1

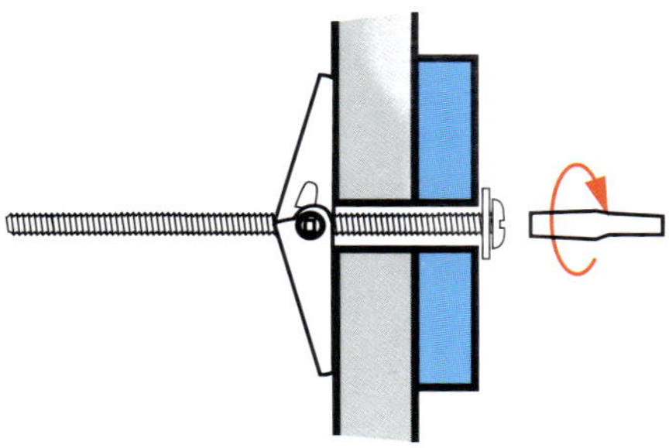

fig. 2

constructed from wooden sheet or plasterboard, behind which is a cavity.

A hole is drilled through the wall large enough for the toggle, with wings folded back, to go through. The object to be fixed is then attached to the toggle and the wing part pushed through the drilled hole. Once through, the wings should spring open and, when the toggle is fastened, pull against the back of the board (fig. 2). If necessary, the wings can be removed, so that the bolt can go through a smaller hole in the object, and then be reattached.

Spring toggles are available in a variety of both length and bolt diameter, depending on the depth of the cavity, the board thickness and the object. They cannot be reused, as once the bolt is undone the toggle will disappear down the cavity.

ANCHOR FIXINGS

Similar to the spring-toggle mechanism, these have a collapsible metal collar that folds back and anchors itself against the back of the board, once inserted and tightened up. It has the advantage, unlike the toggle, that the object can be removed and reattached, or prefixed. Their one disadvantage is that they are difficult to remove when you're trying to make good.

ANCHOR FIXING

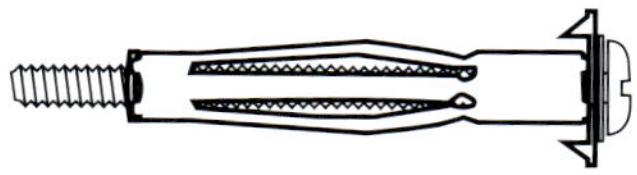

HSS bit or

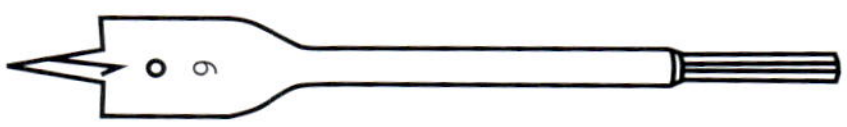

flat bit

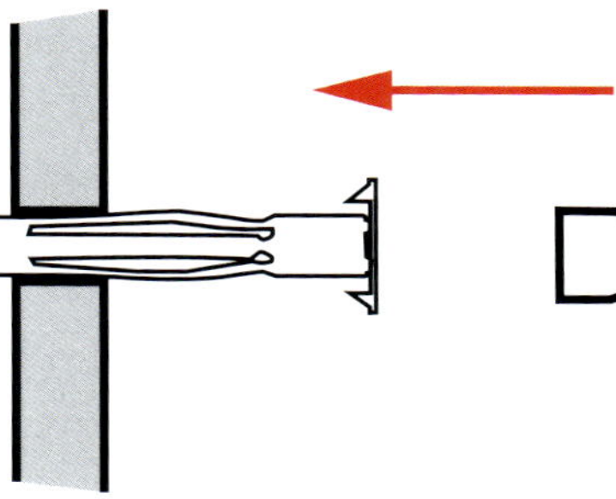

fig. 1

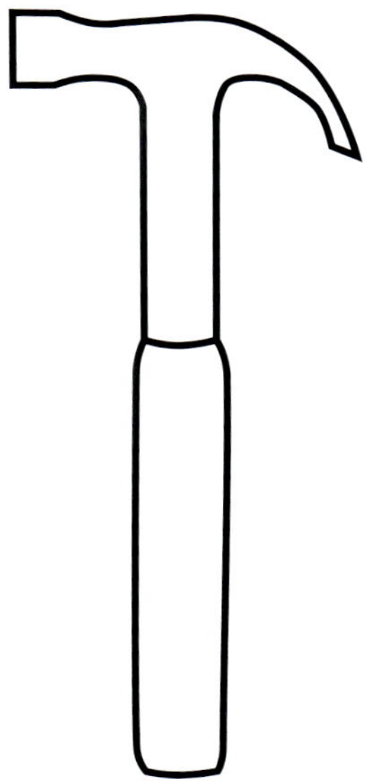

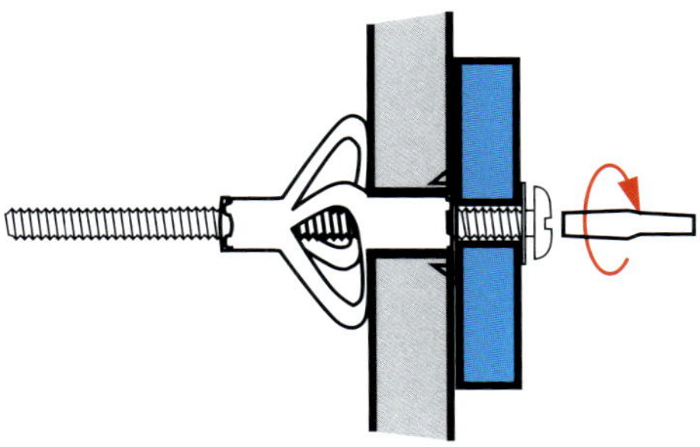

fig. 2

RAWLBOLTS (SHIELD-ANCHOR BOLT)

These are probably the most versatile heavy-duty fixing for hanging heavy loads on masonry walls, ceilings and floors. They come in several forms and sizes (see diagrams). For most purposes M6 or M8 bolts should suffice.

The bolts are mechanically held in the hole by 'setting'. This is the action whereby the wedge at the end of the bolt is pulled back through the fixing, as the nut is tightened. This opens the 'shields', forcing them outwards to lock into the hole (see fig. 3).

When drilling the holes, use a masonry bit that is 6 mm larger than the size of bolt:

M6 bolt	12 mm (1/2 in.) drill bit
	10 mm (3/8 in.) nut
M8 bolt	14 mm (9/16 in.) drill bit
	17 mm (11/16 in.) nut
M10 bolt	16 mm (5/8 in.) drill bit
	21 mm (13/16 in.) nut

The bolt size refers to the threaded bolt, not the shield.

It's a good idea to clean out the hole with blower or brush, though in practice you can use the drill to pull out the debris.

It is sometimes preferable to set the bolt before attaching the object; this is done by tightening the nut. Once set, the bolt can be removed, the object positioned and the bolt retightened. Otherwise it can be set with the object attached. Remember that when setting the eye or hook types you should tighten up with the

RAWLBOLT – INSTALLATION

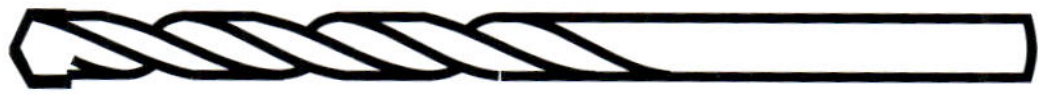

masonry bit

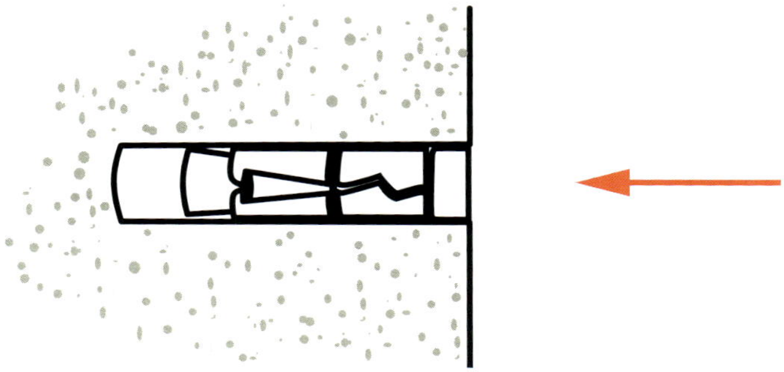

fig. 1

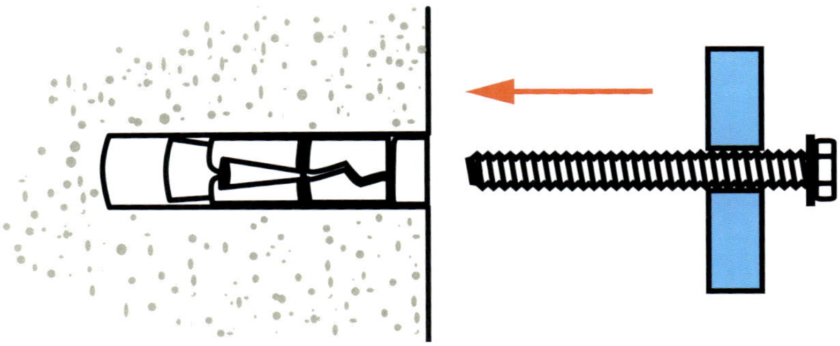

fig. 2

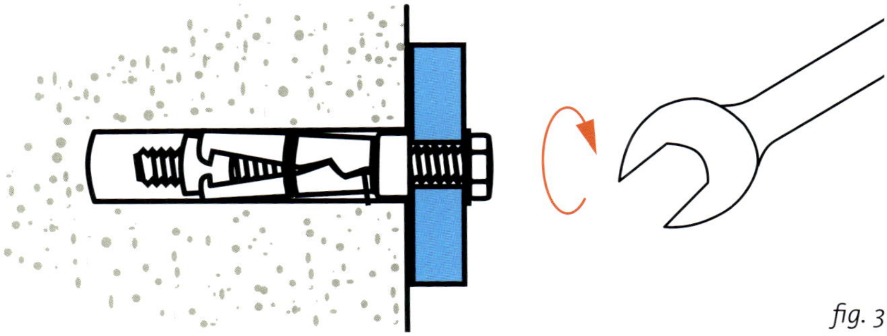

fig. 3

nut, for which you will need a spanner or socket driver (see Spanners, page 75).

When buying, be careful to get the right type. Obviously, the ones with a hook or eye are particularly useful for rigging (suspending objects from cable, etc.). If using the loose or projecting bolt type, make sure that the bolt is long enough to go through both, i.e. the fixing itself and the object or component being secured (plus, of course, the nut and washer). The loose bolt types are particularly useful, as you can insert any bolt of the same size (i.e. M6 or M8) and any length (see illustration in Nuts and bolts, page 74); in the projecting bolt type, the wedge and bolt are one, so this is not possible.

There are also various chemical bolts on the market. These are bolts that are set into the hole with resin. They should not be used for exhibition purposes, as they are virtually impossible to remove.

SPECIALIST FIXINGS

There is a whole world of fixings out there; I've just covered the basics, which hopefully should suffice in most cases. If you get stuck, try Googling manufacturers' websites, such as Fischer and Rawl, or go to a good builder's merchant for further advice (see the back of this guide for websites).

Of course, you can always improvise – I once hung a friend's work on a drill bit!

RAWLBOLT TYPES

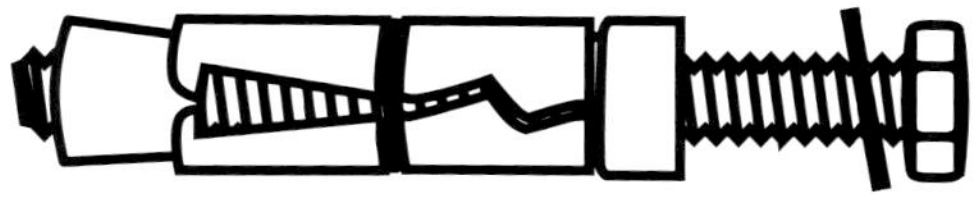

Loose bolt

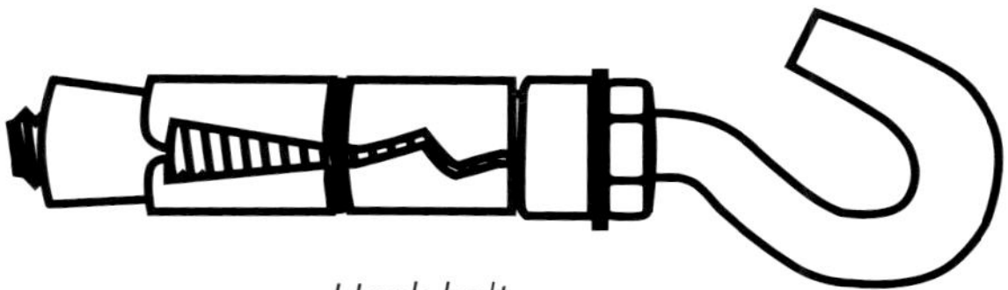

Hook bolt

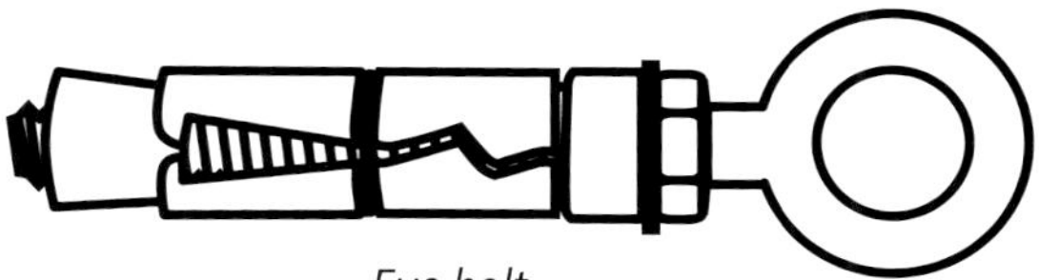

Eye bolt

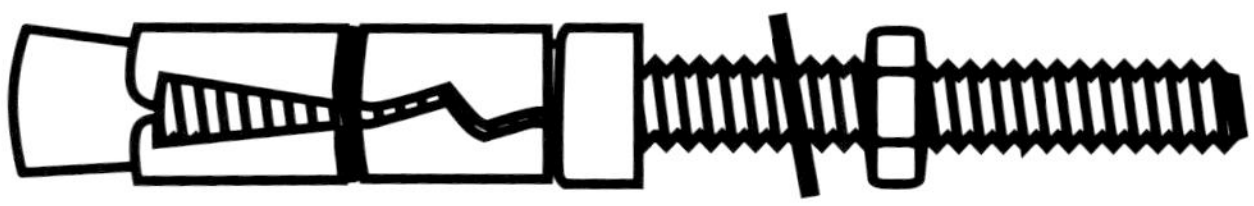

Projecting bolt

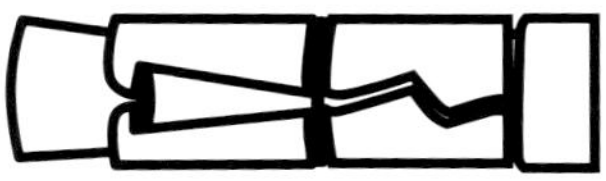

Shield only

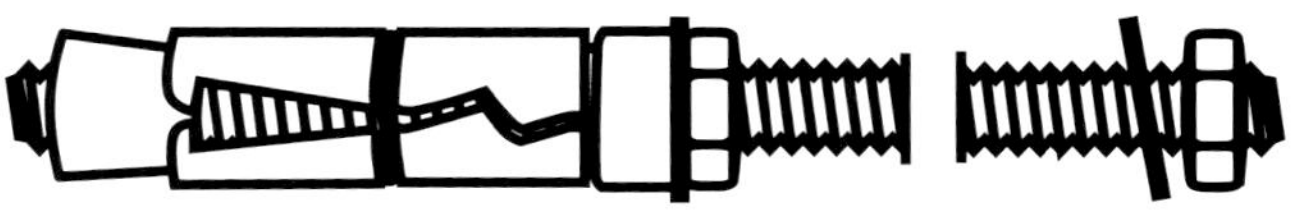

Shield with studding

NUTS & BOLTS

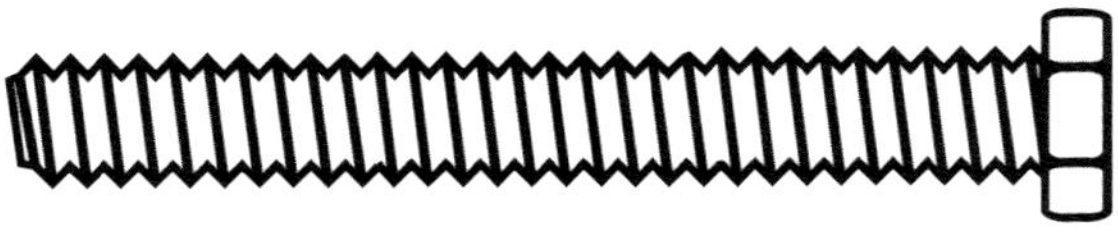

Bolt

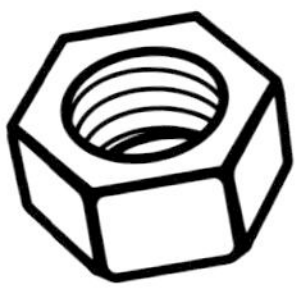

Nut

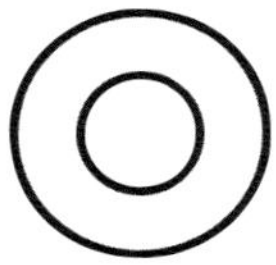

Washer

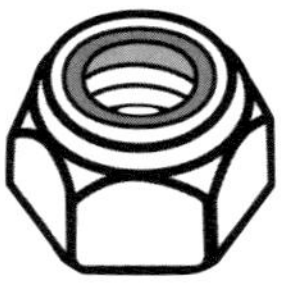

Nylon locknut

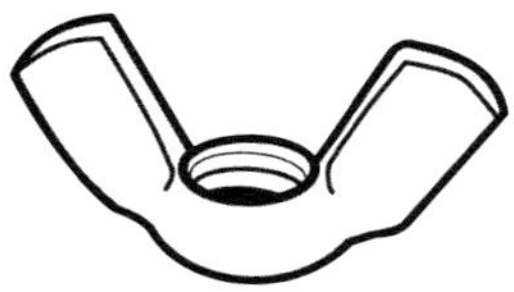

Wing nut

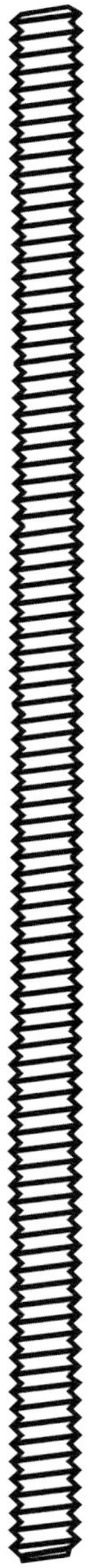

Studding

SPANNERS, ETC.

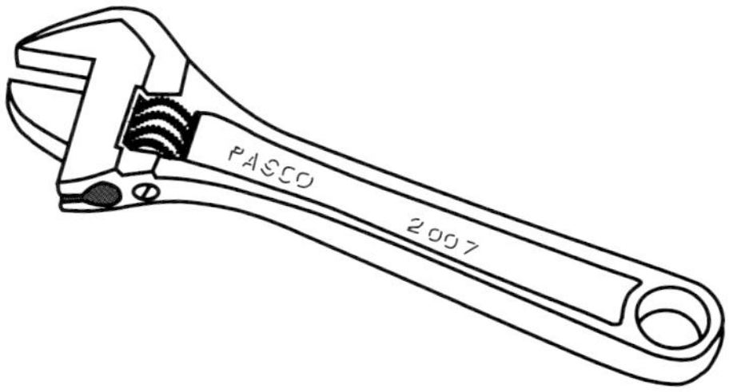

Adjustable wrench

Open-ended spanner

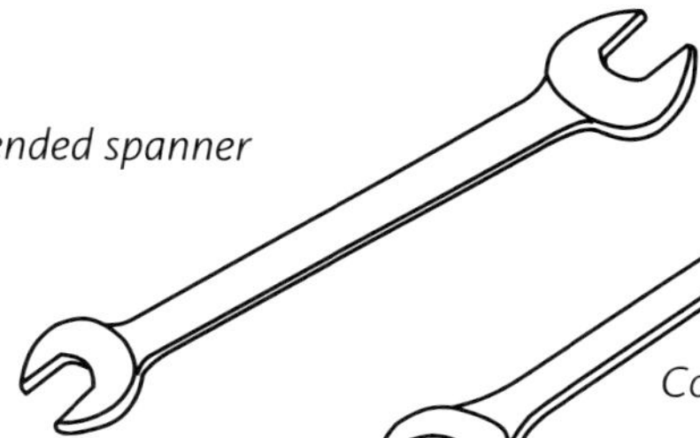

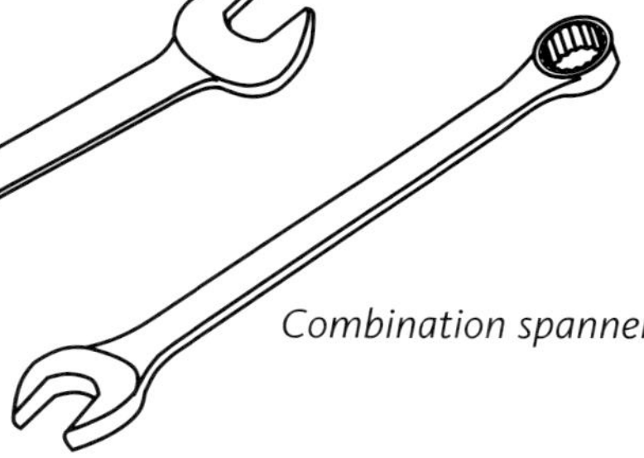

Combination spanner (open + ring)

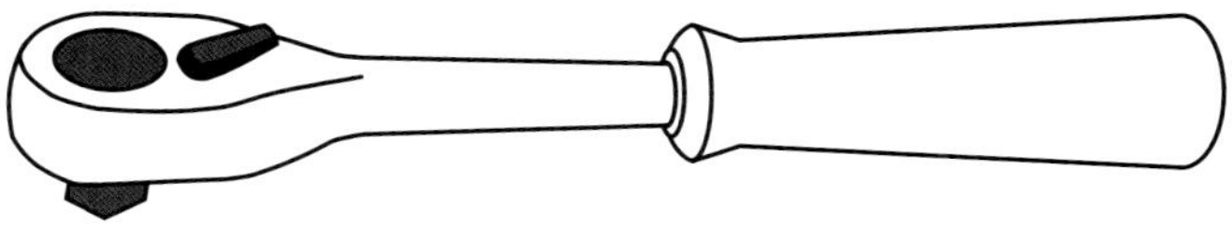

Socket driver with ratchet

Sockets

5

stage five

two-dimensional work

HANGING 2-DIMENSIONAL WORK

notes

PLANNING

Think about what you want to show. How many paintings/photographs/drawings do you want to fit into the space? What sort of hang is it going to be? Are they going to be spaced out or grouped together? Do you need to frame anything? Don't leave things to the last minute – be realistic. If you need to get work framed, mounted professionally and/or printed, allow plenty of time before the show to get this done. I would advise at least a month, if not six weeks. Also, remember to budget properly, as it can be expensive.

SETTING OUT

Once the space is prepared and cleared of all unnecessary items (see Preparation of Space, page 35), the work can be brought into the space and you can start thinking about how it should be placed. You can simply lean it up against the walls, to get an initial impression. Allow plenty of time for the whole hanging process. It's good practice to reflect on decisions, to leave the space and come back refreshed for a second or even third look. Don't be afraid to change things around.

It is advisable that work is installed by at least two people. Juggling screwdrivers and drills whilst trying to level and hold work isn't easy and could lead to disasters. When moving work, remember to hold it firmly on each side, or from top and bottom. Never pick up the work from the top, particularly framed work, as this can stress the mitre joints and loosen the glazing. If possible, wear white cotton gloves when moving unframed work.

notes

EYE LEVEL

The next consideration is eye level, i.e. the height from the ground at which the work will be hung. There are no set rules for this, although interestingly the British Council, who send work abroad, stipulate that the centre of the work should be 156 cm (61 in.) above floor level. This is in my opinion a little high; around 150 cm (59 in.) is more common.

Some work may look better hung higher or lower – e.g., if a work has a particular focal point which isn't central, or if a piece has a relationship with the floor. The size of the available space may also have a bearing on the eye level. If the space is shared, then a consensus needs to be reached. Again, if it doesn't feel right, don't be afraid to change things even once they're hung.

SEQUENCES

There are several ways to hang sequences of work:

fig. 1 Shows several pieces the same size, and the eye level is at the centre point.

fig. 2 Different-sized pieces are hung with the eye level at the centre.

fig. 3 Different-sized work is hung with the tops level. Decide on the eye level for the whole line or choose one piece and work from that.

fig. 4 Again, different-sized work, this time with the bottoms level. This tends to look rather scrappy, a bit like teeth, and is not generally used or recommended.

EYE LEVELS/SEQUENCES

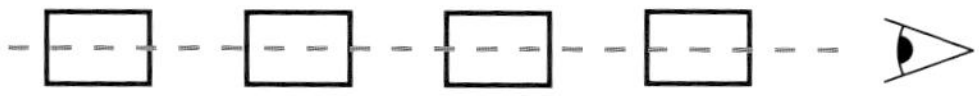

fig. 1

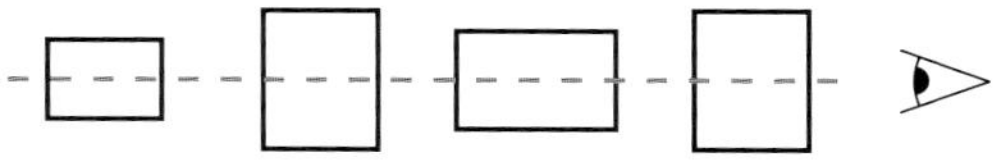

fig.2

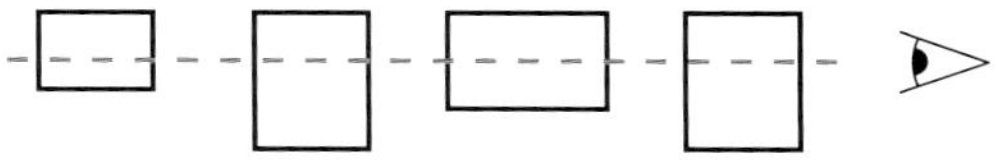

fig. 3

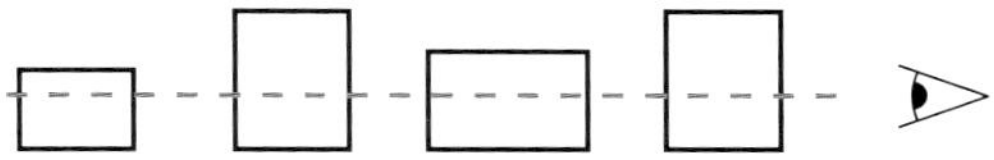

fig. 4

EYE LEVELS/GRIDS

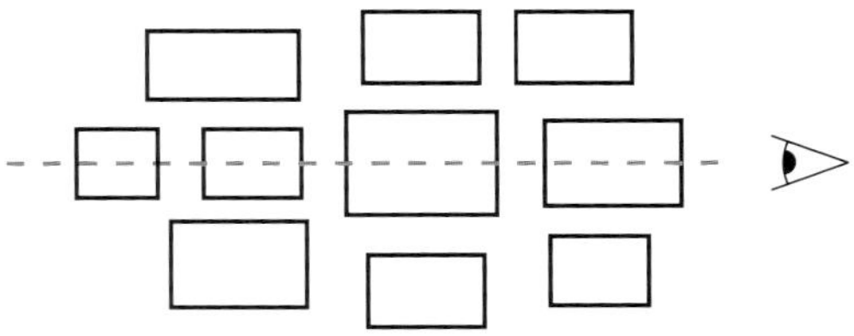

fig. 5

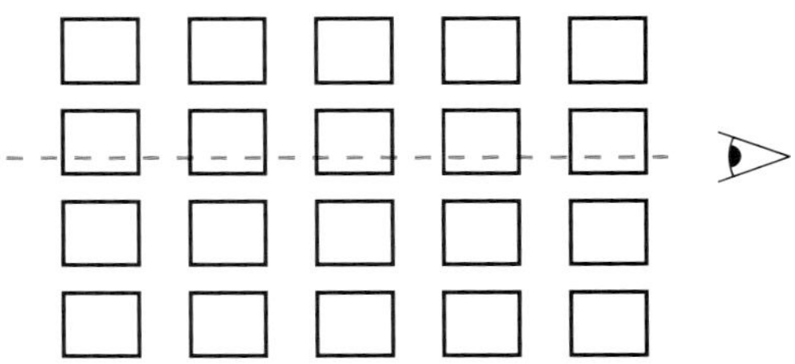

fig. 6

GRIDS

fig. 5 Shows an irregular grid, and here it's probably best to start with the central work and move outwards.

fig. 6 Shows a regular grid. Consider the size and how it fits on the wall to determine the eye level.

NB It may be worth using a paper pattern or mock-up to work out what sort of grid or sequence works best.

HANGING SEQUENCES

You don't want the work to be lost in corners, to be distracted by doorways/openings, or confused by the close proximity of other people's work, so in these circumstances allow extra space. Also take into consideration visual distractions such as light switches or other architectural features. These don't have to be negative – you should accept the fact that they are there and work with them. Fire extinguishers/blankets or signs cannot be moved.

To start marking out the position of the work you will need a tape measure and spirit level, as well as screwdrivers and a drill.

If you are showing work in sequence or on a grid, some basic mathematics is needed to work out the size of the gap (see fig. 7).

- Measure the length of the wall or allotted space (A).

HANGING SEQUENCES

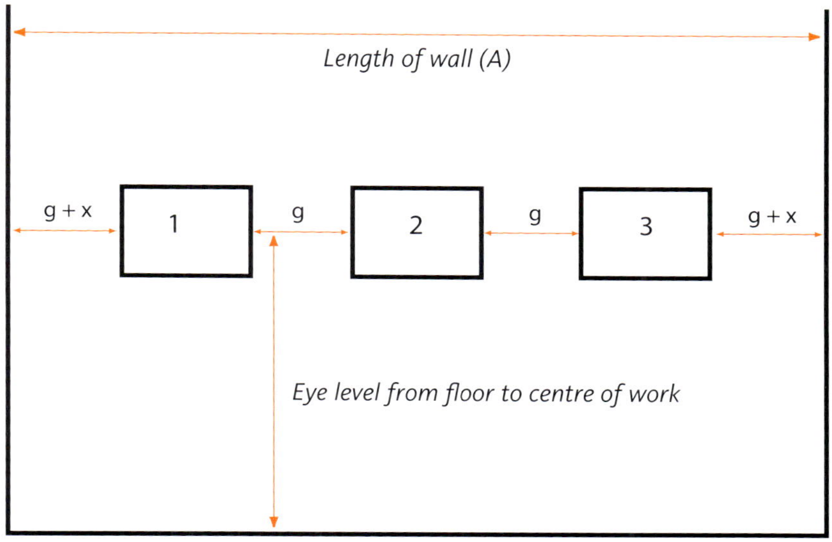

fig. 7

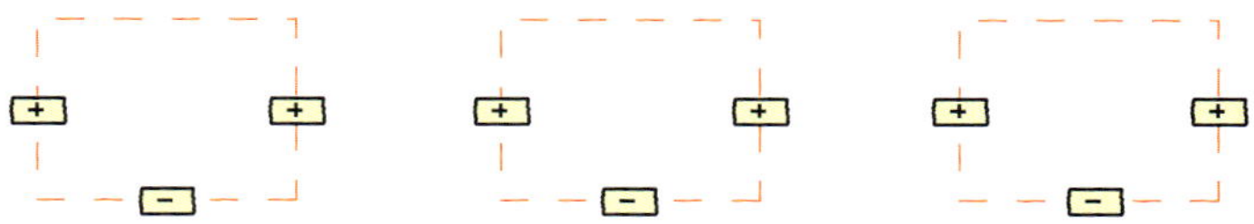

fig. 8

- Measure each work and add together their combined widths (1 + 2 + 3 = B).
- Subtract B from A = C.
- Divide this by the number of gaps (number of works + 1); remember, you may need to add a little onto the gaps at the ends (g + x), allowing for corners, etc.
- This will give the size of the gap between each work.

MARKING

Rather than marking the wall with pencil marks which you will later have to erase or paint over, it's best to use masking tape, which is stuck to the wall in the necessary places and can then be marked (fig. 8). Some people use cotton thread to define levels and positions. If a standard height is required, a pre-marked stick can be used to give the eye level.

SPIRIT LEVEL

Whichever method you decide to use to hang your work, you should always use a spirit level (see Basic Tools, page 13) to gauge both horizontals and verticals. Remember that sometimes, despite the spirit level showing that the work is level, it may not always appear so. This can be a result of the floor, walls or corners not being absolutely true (they rarely are), or because of other visual distractions. Don't be afraid to tweak the levels using the naked eye.

HANGING DEVICES

MIRROR/PICTURE PLATES

Mirror plates, or picture plates, are a standard

MIRROR PLATES

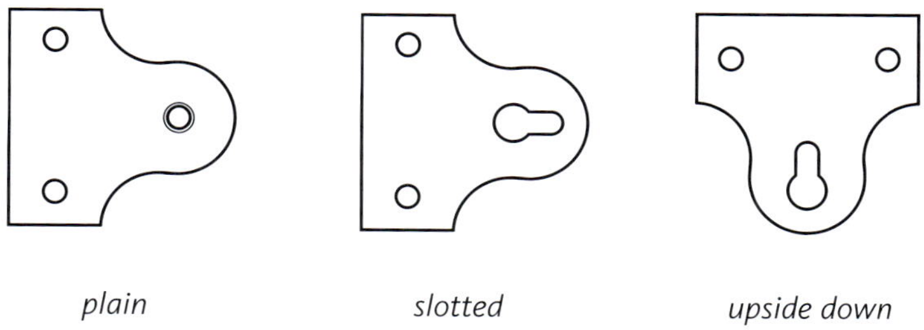

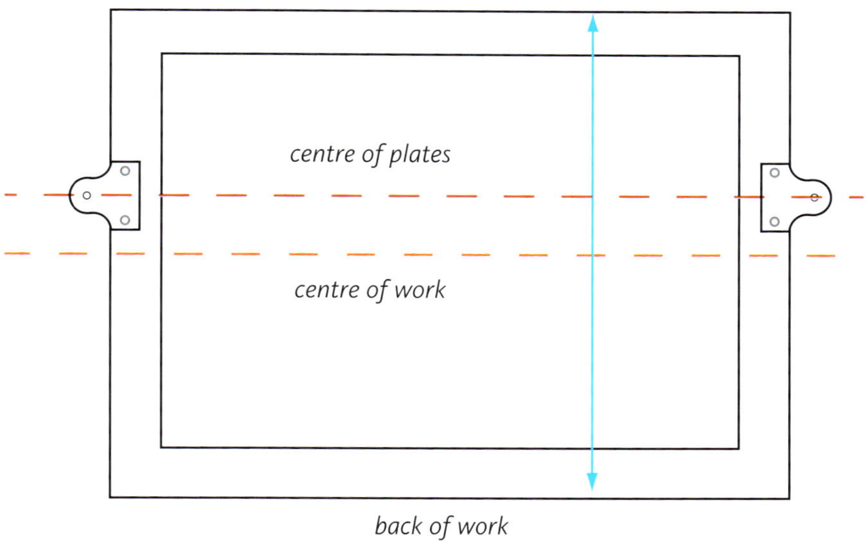

fig. 1

way of hanging framed work, stretchers and rigid supports. They have the advantage of being easy to use – the work is held flat against the wall – and they offer some security. They are, however, visible (except for the upside down plate, see diagram), which may not be to everyone's taste. To make them less obvious they can be painted over to match the wall, or taped over then painted. It might be wise, in some instances, to pre-paint them before attaching them to the work. They are generally brass, or brass-plated (it's a shame no one has yet thought to anodise them white), and come in various sizes. Obviously, the larger the work the larger the plate will have to be. The screw holes are usually countersunk.

Generally, a pair of plates will suffice, one on either side of the frame. There is a rule, although I would not say it is set in stone, that the height of the mirror plate should be halfway + 10% of the height (see fig. 1). Attach the plates to the back of the work (see fig. 2), using the appropriate-sized screw. Make sure when doing this you don't damage the actual work – use packing material, etc. to protect the front.

To avoid drilling through to the front of the frame or picture surface, wrap a piece of tape (see fig. 2) around the drill bit so that you know when to stop.

Hand drills are really good for this, as they are more controllable (see Basic Tools, page 13).

Once the plates are positioned, the work can be turned around and hung as follows:

MIRROR PLATES

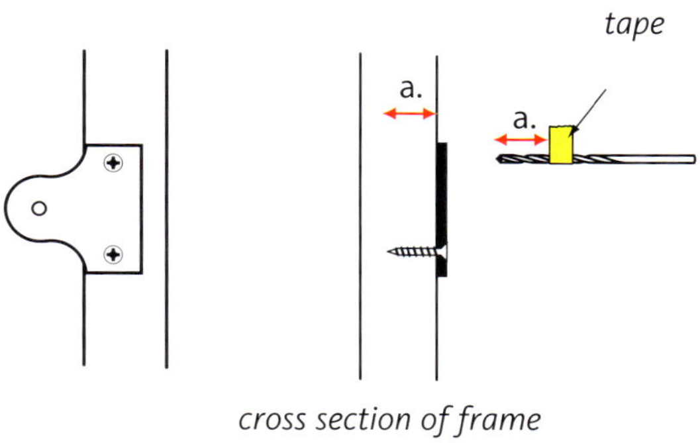

fig. 2

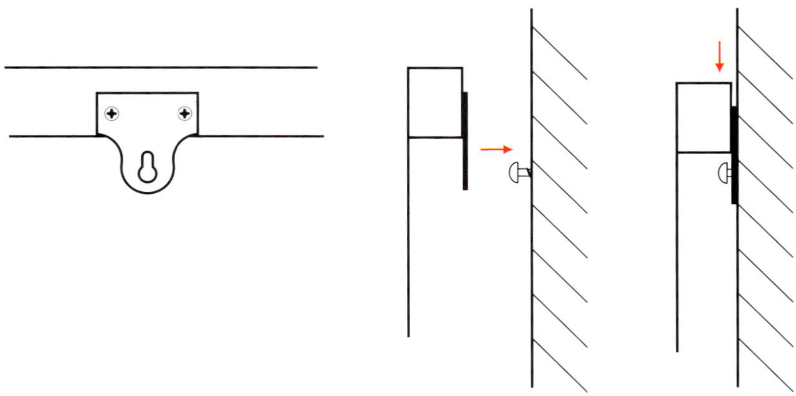

fig. 3

- Offer up the work, level and mark through the hole on the plate on one side.
- Remove the work to a safe place.
- Drill a hole where marked and use a suitable fixing, i.e. a Rawlplug, if required.

TIP: if you're drilling into masonry, an open envelope can be taped to the wall underneath the hole to catch the resultant dust.

- Reposition the work. Screw through the plate into the hole.
- Using a spirit level and your eye, mark through the second plate.
- Remove the work from the wall, drill as before, and then re-hang. This may seem tedious but it does avoid damage to the work.

Some large work may need two plates on either side, in which case it's best to place these at positions equidistant from top and bottom. Occasionally, it may be necessary to put plates at the top; to avoid stress on the frame these should be balanced out with plates at the bottom. It might be easier in this case to use slotted plates at the top (see diagram); the screws (which should be round-headed) can be pre-positioned and the painting 'dropped' in, with the bottom plates screwed in last.

Upside-down plates can be used on the backs of frames where there is a recess, such as with stretched-canvas frames. It is not advisable to

SPLIT BATTENS

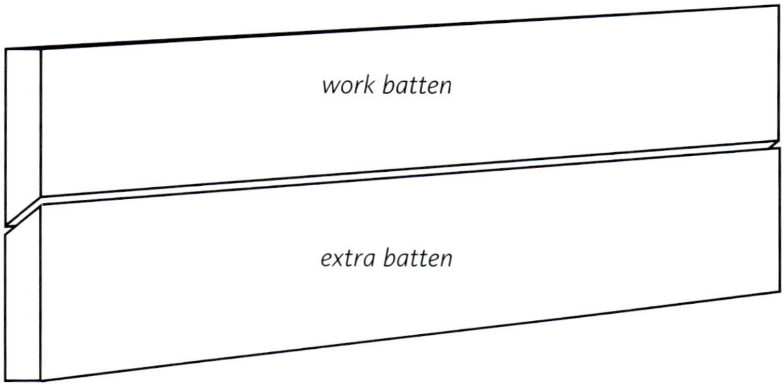

fig. 1

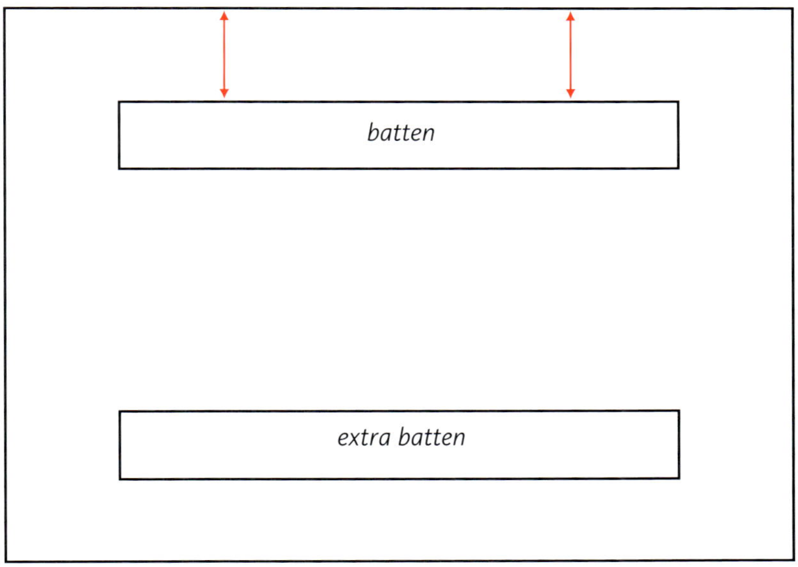

back of work

fig. 2

use these plates on glazed items, as they could stress the frame. They do require careful measuring and marking out, as you have to 'drop' the plates onto pre-positioned screws. As with the standard slotted plates, round-headed screws should be used (see fig. 3). Although slightly awkward to use – it can be difficult to match up the screws to the holes – they do have the advantage of being invisible. They are best used in pairs so as to avoid tilting.

SPLIT BATTENS

Split battens are simple devices that offer a very effective means of hanging work. They are made from thin strips of wood – usually sheet wood, though MDF is ideal – which have been cut lengthways at a 45–60° angle (see fig. 1). One piece is fixed to the back of the work, the other to the wall. A flat hook has been created by the angle at which the battens have been cut, allowing the work to sit securely on the wall (see fig. 2). Because the batten is fixed to the back of the work, when attached to the wall the work 'floats'. How much gap there is between the wall and the back of the piece obviously depends on the thickness of the batten.

Fixing

The batten is fixed to the back of the work and, importantly, must be parallel with the top (fig. 2). If you're using wood supports for the work, then the batten can be glued in place. Countersunk screws can also be used, though use a piece of tape on the drill bit as a guide (see mirror plate diagrams), to make sure you don't drill through to the front.

If your work is mounted on aluminium or a similar material, glue on the batten with a two-part resin glue such as Araldite (aircraft tape is sometimes used). If you're getting the work professionally

SPLIT BATTENS

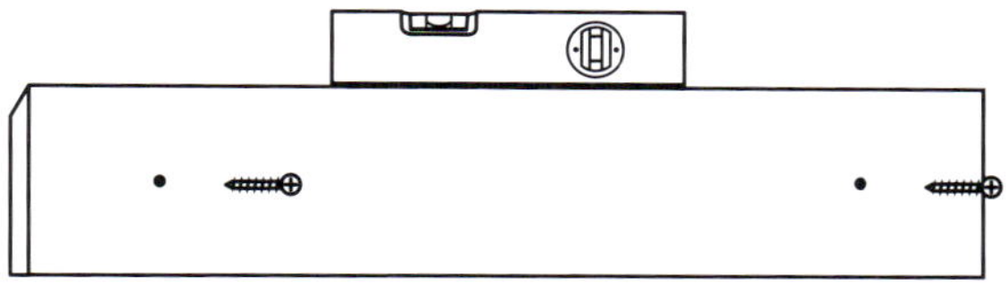

fig. 3

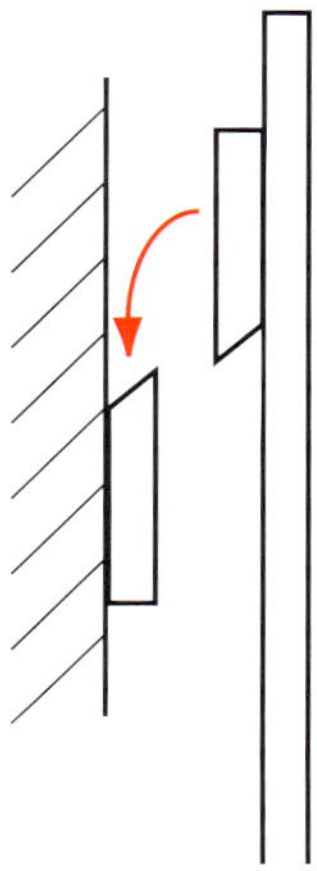

fig. 4

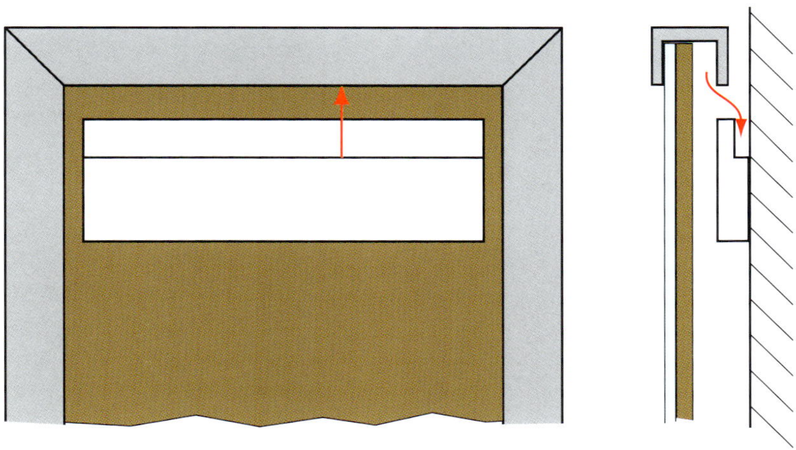

back of work

fig. 5

mounted, you should be able to ask for split battens to be fixed as part of the process.
Make the battens shorter than the width of the work, so they cannot be seen.

On larger work it's advisable to fix an extra batten near the bottom to avoid any leaning in. This needn't be angled.

Fix the batten to the wall, using a spirit level to make sure it's horizontal (fig. 3).

The work can then be 'dropped' in (fig. 4).

If the work needs any slight realignment, small slivers of matchstick/wood can be used as wedges between the battens.

ALTERNATIVE BATTENS

The split-batten concept can be adapted to suit other types of work. Figs. 5–9 show some alternatives.

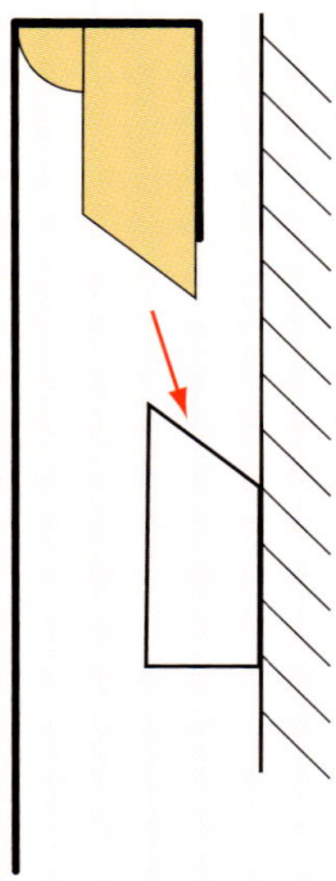

fig. 6

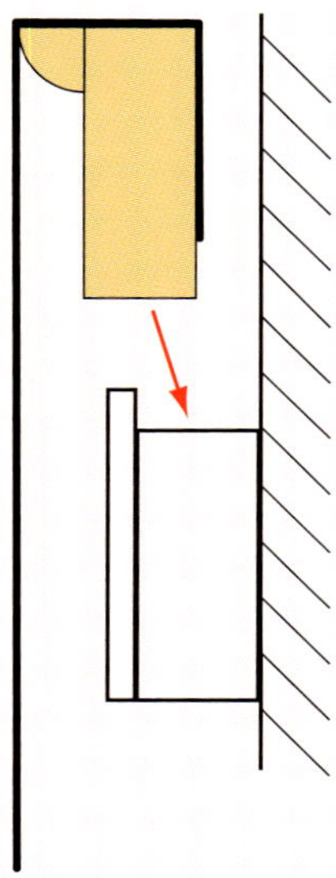

fig. 7

BATTENS

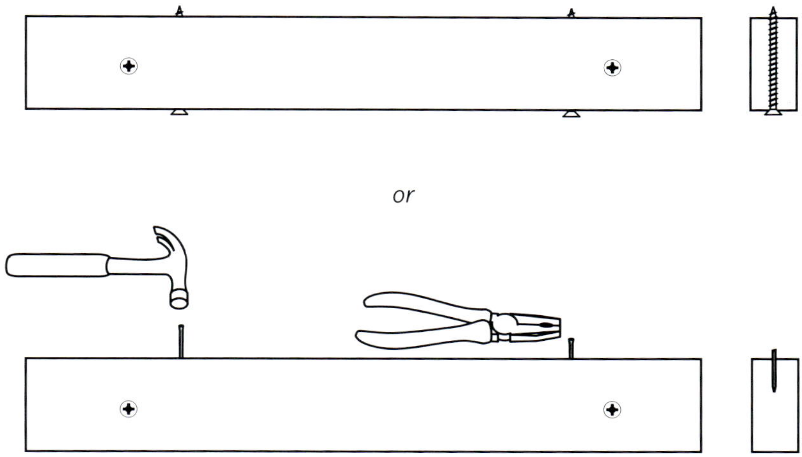

fig. 8

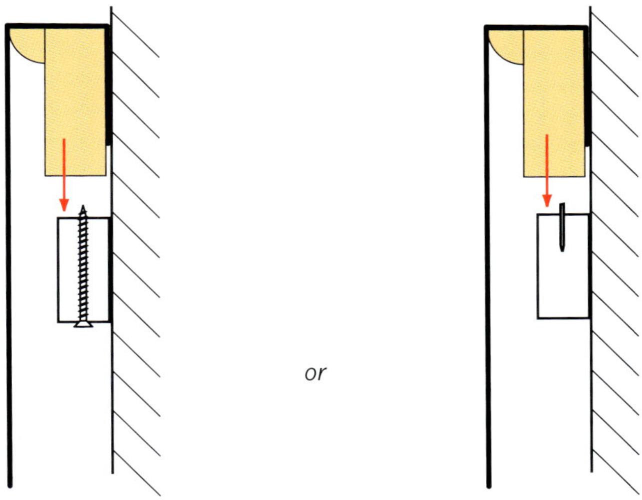

fig. 9

HANGING WITH SCREWS

Using screws directly is both a common and a quick method of hanging paintings on stretchers. I would always use screws in preference to nails, as the vibrations from hammering can dislodge any work – yours or someone else's – in the immediate vicinity. They can also be used in masonry walls with the aid of Rawlplugs™. I would never use masonry nails.

Having decided the position of the piece, mark out and position two screws. The screws need to be far enough apart to provide a stable platform, and should also be positioned below the top height of the work (fig. 1). Measure the depth of the top bar of the frame or stretcher, distance X, and deduct this from the top height. The screws are then screwed in so that they sit inside the stretcher bar (fig. 2).

Alternatively, with paintings, sit the top bar on top of the screw head, and gently push the painting down onto the head to give a firmer grip, or make a shallow groove in the underside of the bar (fig. 3).

HANGING WITH SCREWS

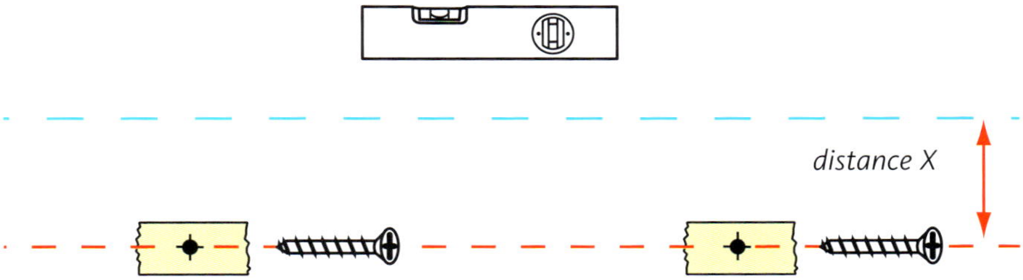

fig. 1

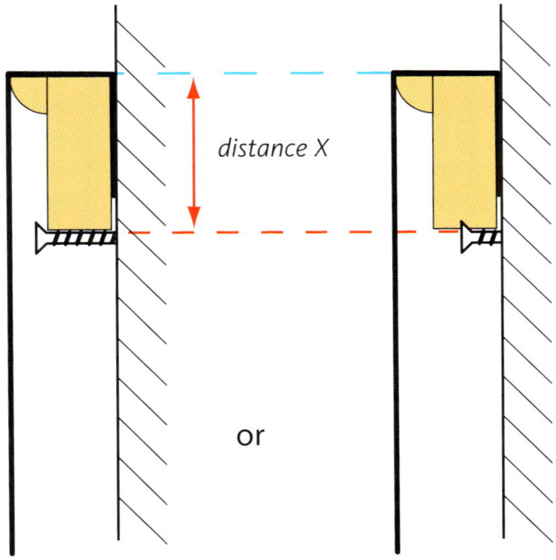

fig. 2

fig. 3

If the painting does not appear level, remove it and tap the screws up or down to adjust (fig. 4).

Small framed work can also be installed in the same manner – you may find alternative screws, such as the washer-head type, are better-suited to this purpose (fig. 5).

This method is not ideal for larger framed work, where the weight of the glass is likely to stress the top mitre joints.

HANGING WITH SCREWS

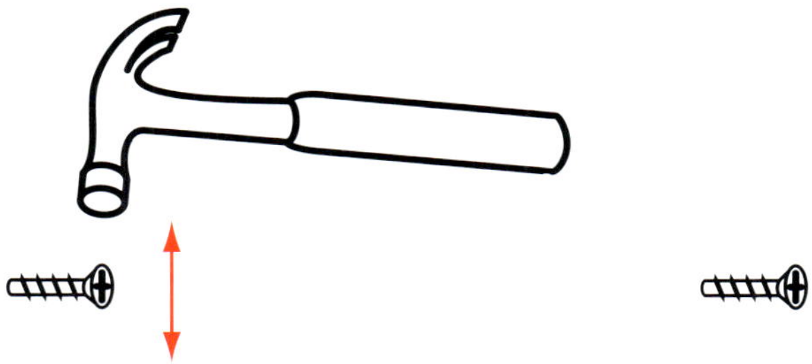

fig. 4

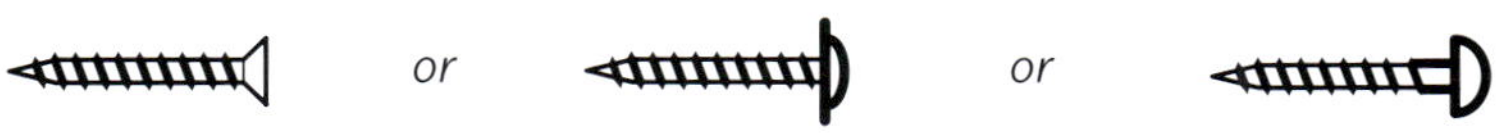

screw alternatives

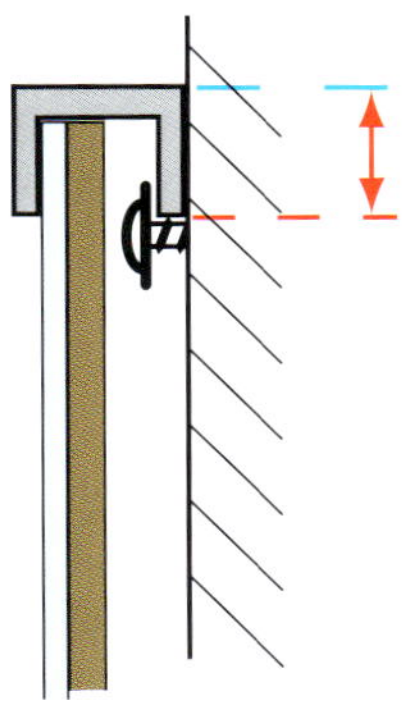

fig. 5

RECESSED CHANNEL

If the work is made on board and needs to be shown flat rather than floating (as in split batons), and you do not want to see the fixings, a recess can be made in the back.

At its simplest this can be a drilled hole, allowing the work to be hung from a single screw. For a more secure fixing a longer channel is made in conjunction with a flat strip of metal, which makes an inverted hook. I usually use aluminium 20 mm ($\frac{3}{4}$ in.) wide x 2 mm ($\frac{1}{12}$ in.) deep, which can be cut to length with a hacksaw.

Recesses should preferably be made during the preparation of the board, but can also be made retrospectively if care is taken with the surface of the work (see figs 1 & 2). A router (a high-speed cutting machine) is the ideal tool for this job, but if this is not available the channel can be drilled out using a Forstner bit (these have the advantage of having a shallow guide tip) and finished off with a sharp chisel. Obviously, care should be taken not to go through to the front of the board, and in this regard you may wish to wrap a piece of tape around the bit to act as a visual guide (see Mirror plates, page 83). The shallow recess to accommodate the metal strip is then chiselled out. Make sure that the recess is parallel to the top of the board. The metal strip can be drilled out and countersunk to allow for small screws to fix it into the back of the board. For extra security the plate can be screwed and glued using a two-part epoxy glue such as Araldite.

RECESSED CHANNEL

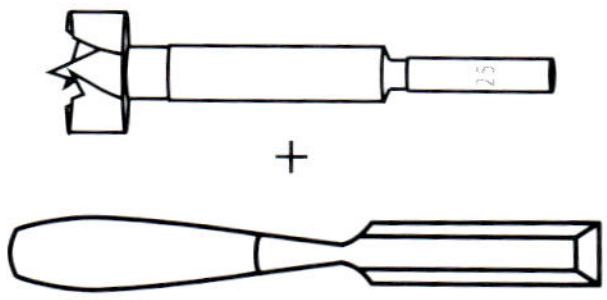

Forstner bit and chisel or router

Hacksaw

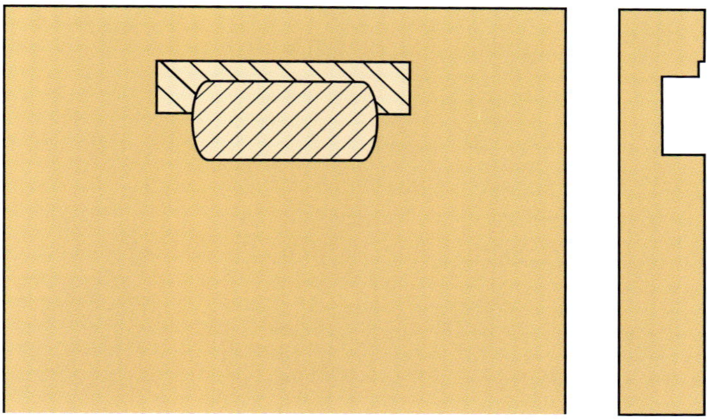

fig. 1

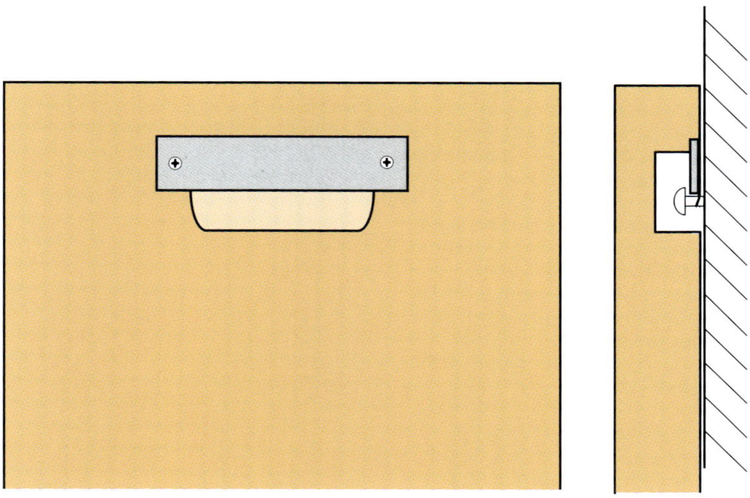

fig. 2

STRAP HANGERS

These are often used for large and/or heavy-framed work, and come in a variety of forms and sizes. They should be screwed into the back of the frame as in fig. 1. The work can then be hung on screws or flat hooks (fig. 2). To make the hanging easier the buckles can be pulled out.

OTHER DEVICES

You will find lots of fixing devices on the market – it is really a question of what works best for you. Do remember that some are made for the domestic market and may appear un-professional – for example, I would not recommend hanging pictures from string or wire, as they tend to hang out from the wall and are easily nudged out of position.

Velcro can be used, though with care. There is a tendency for people to use too little; don't skimp, as you are likely to find your work on the floor if you do. I would recommend stapling Velcro to walls, if possible. It should only be used for relatively light work.

SECURITY

There are various security fixings available. They tend to be fairly specialist and are used by galleries and institutions where security is an issue. They will usually require specific tools for the fixing.

The best security is to have the show invigilated, something that should always be considered during planning.

STRAP HANGERS

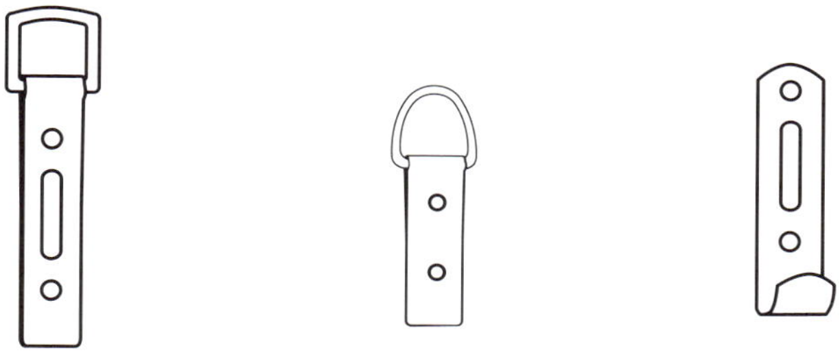

strap hangers *hook*

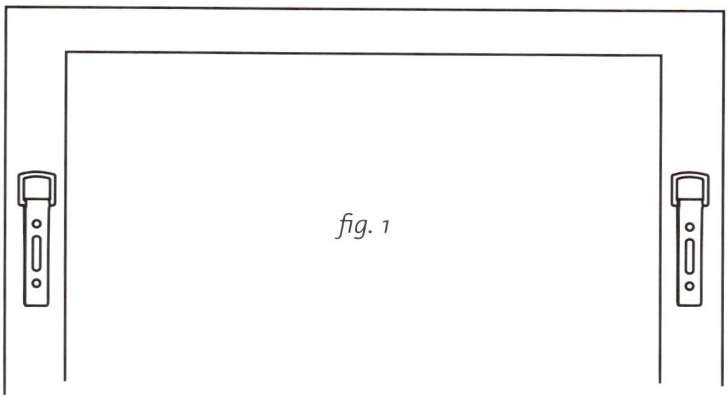

fig. 1

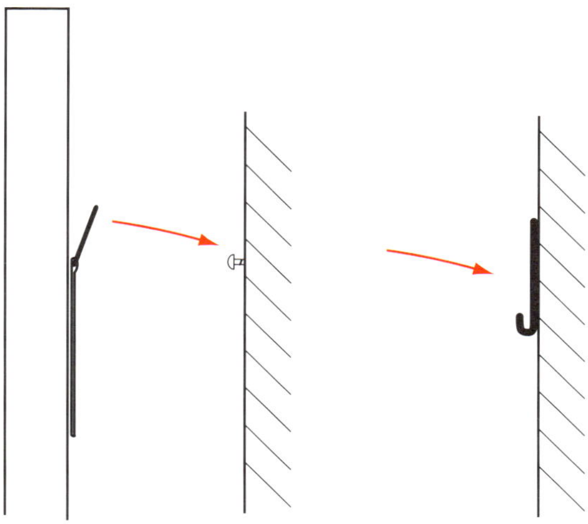

fig. 2

ALTERNATIVES

When I go and see shows, out of habit I look at the way things are installed and take note, particularly if a slightly different approach than the norm is taken.

I've shown three examples, seen recently or that I've used myself, which in their context have worked well. They all involve adapting items designed for other uses to suit this purpose.

The cable clips were used to show unframed drawings with a Perspex or glass cover. As the diagram shows, they are trimmed to make a flat hook. Cable clips come in a variety of sizes and colours, so you can decide which will work best.

Dresser hooks, seen at a recent show of paintings on board, were adapted by adding a clear plastic sleeve to cover the hook part, to protect the painting surface.

Panel pins were used to hang small, unframed photographs that were sandwiched between a sheet of glass and a piece of board.

All these methods require a degree of accuracy and care; in this regard, I would suggest that the works are marked up and the holes pre-drilled (see fig. 1). The bottom pins or hooks can then be tapped or screwed in before you position the work (fig. 2). Finally, put in the top pins (fig. 3). The dresser hooks can be turned in once the work is in place.

ALTERNATIVES

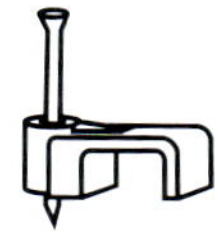

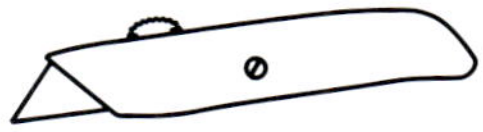

cable clips

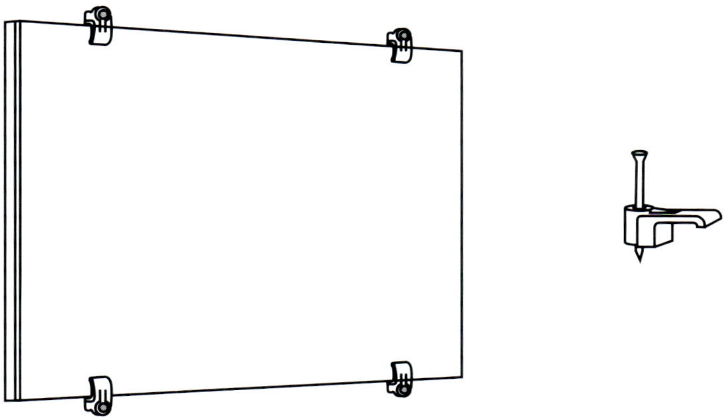

dresser hooks

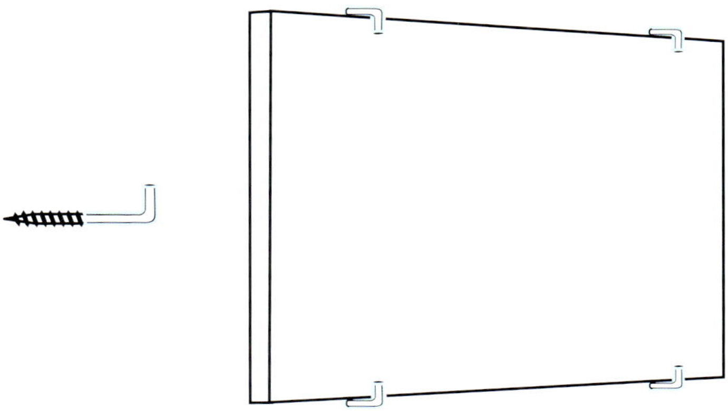

ALTERNATIVES

Panel pins

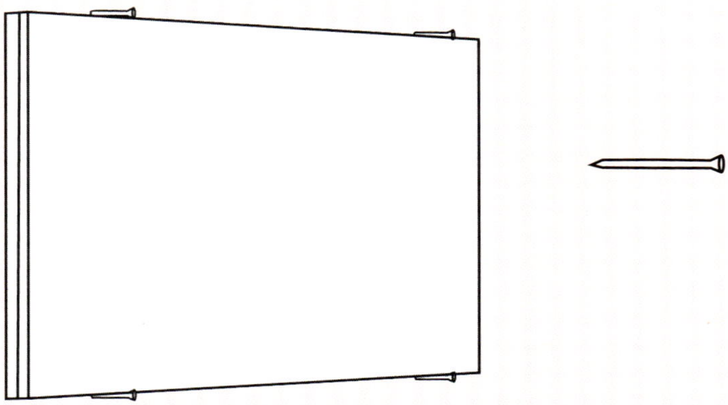

using panel pins

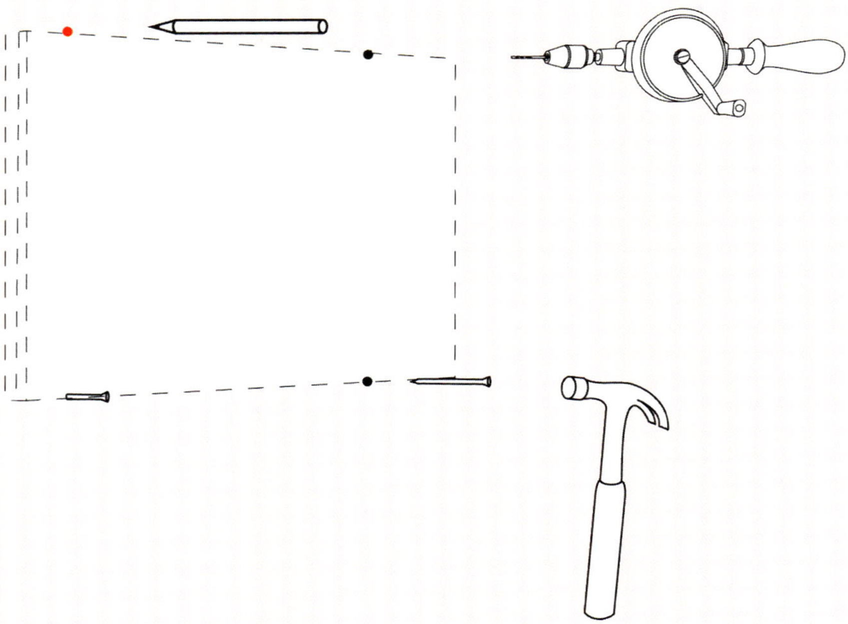

fig. 1

USING PANEL PINS

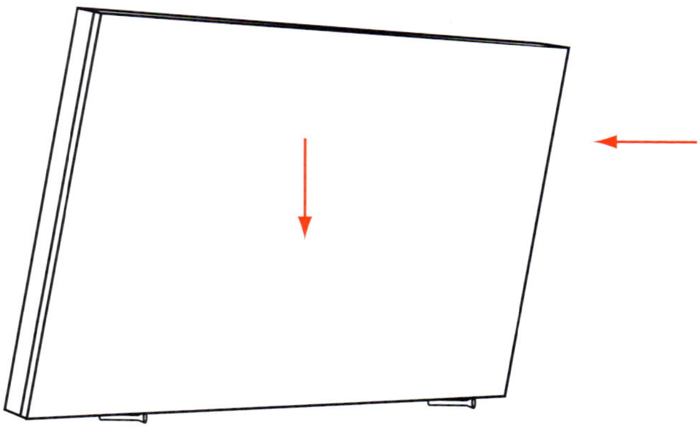

fig. 2

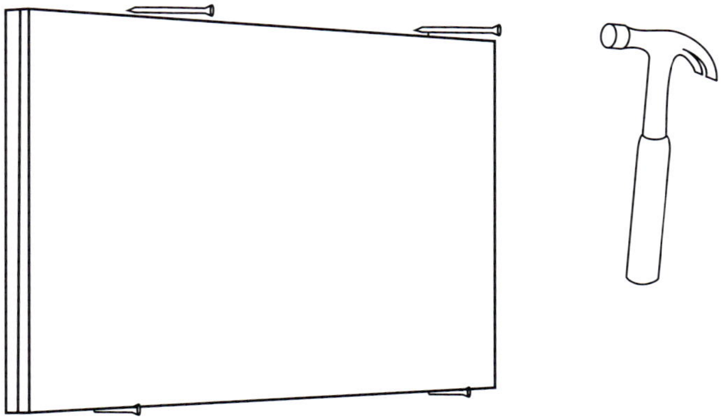

fig. 3

PAPER WORKS

Paper works are quite often shown unframed. This is perfectly acceptable, but it does pose problems as to how to hang without causing damage to the work. Remember that edges will tend to get worn and torn. How precious are you about your work? Does it need to last for more than one show?

Consider the type of paper you are using:

- If it isn't acid-free, then it will gradually turn yellow and eventually decompose

- If the drawings are on a large scale, think about using heavier-grade paper

- It's common for people to use 'easy' solutions, but these are not recommended.

Here is a list of what NOT to use:

Blu-tack
Masking tape
Double-sided tape
Sellotape
Sticky Fixers

And here are the reasons why not:

- All the above are either greasy or acidic, and thus are likely to mark the paper

- They are likely to damage the paper surface when they are removed

- They tend to fail, meaning your work will fall off the wall

- They can be difficult to remove from the wall

- It's basically unprofessional to use them, for all of the above reasons!

There are a number of solutions, which will not only help to conserve the work, but will add to the professional feeling of the hang.

Corners can be strengthened with linen tape. This is a non-acidic, non-marking tape that is stuck onto the back of the paper with a small amount of water; the process is also reversible i.e. you can take it off again, which may be handy. You can buy it in rolls and cut it to size.

Once they are strong enough, there are a number of ways to hang the drawings:

- Pinning – there is a huge choice of pins out there: dressmaking pins, mapping pins, panel pins, etc. Select those which are most suitable for the work. If it's difficult to get the pins into the wall, you can always drill small holes. Even putting pins into masonry is not impossible; you can drill a small hole using a masonry bit and then stuff it with as many matchstick slivers as the hole allows.

- Gripping devices – such as bulldog clips. These are worth using, provided you place foam pads between the face of the clip and the drawing.

- Hanging bar – this should be fixed to the top of the paper, though it is best to sandwich the paper between two bars, as this will keep the work centred. You would then possibly need to attach a similar bar to the bottom to avoid the paper curling.

- Eyelets – these can work well, especially with larger work, but make sure you get decent ones (stainless steel or brass), as they can rust.

- Linen tape – the tape itself can be used as a hanging device. Fig. 2 shows it being used as a V-hinge. Cut the tape to size, and fold to form the hinge. Apply to the back of the paper work, then fix to the wall. An additional strip can be put across the wall half of the hinge. Decide on the position or height of the work and mark the position of the top corners on the wall prior to fixing, so that you have a guide.

- Pasting drawings or printed works directly on to the wall – obviously a one-off. Check out the condition of the wall and prepare as necessary. It may be a good idea to prime the wall with the paste before applying the work; a good-quality wallpaper paste can be used for this, though remember to check that the material components of the work you want to hang will withstand getting wet. In this regard, it is probably a good idea to practise with the same kind of material, prior to pasting the final piece.

PAPER WORKS

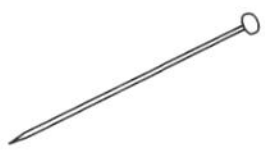

pin

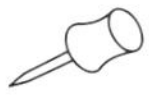

mapping pin

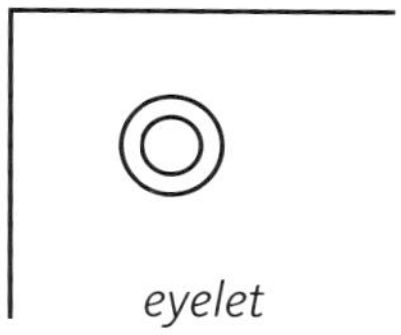

eyelet

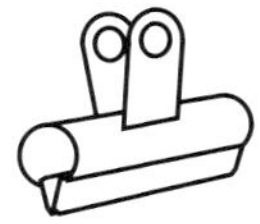

bulldog clip

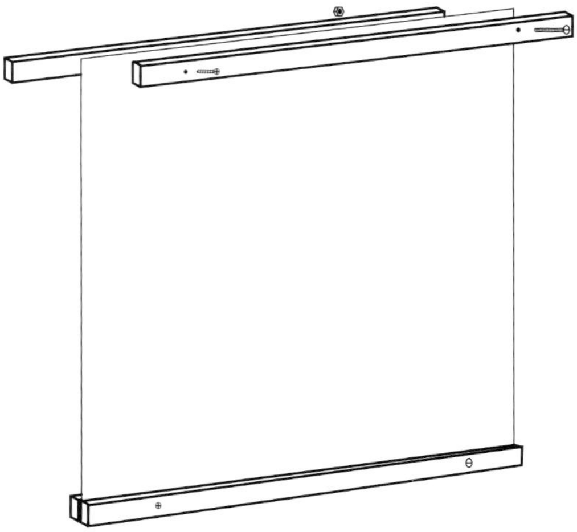

fig. 1

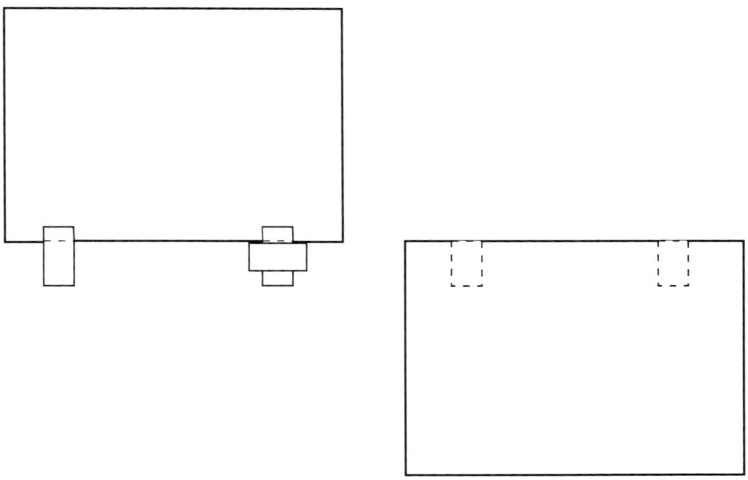

fig. 2

6

stage six

rigging

RIGGING

notes

Wire cable provides a good way of suspending objects, screens, etc. from the ceiling. It can also be stretched across spaces and has the advantage that, because it can be tensioned, it won't sag.

Cable is made from several bundles of multi-stranded wire. You can buy either galvanised or stainless steel wire; I recommend stainless steel, as it looks better and is easier to use. It's available in a range of diameters and bundle configurations (see tables below). The most flexible is 7 x 19, i.e. the cable is made up of 7 bundles, each of which has 19 strands. Thinner cable may be sold in 7 x 7, which is still flexible. It is recommended that you use cable that will take five times the load, e.g. if you are hanging an object that weighs 50 kg (23 lb), use cable that has a breaking load of at least 250 kg (550 lb).

Breaking load of stainless-steel wire, 7 x 19, 316 grade (guide only); AWG stands for American Wire Gauge:

2.00 mm (AWG 12)	225 kg (500 lb)
2.5 mm (AWG 10)	350 kg (770 lb)
3.0 mm (AWG 9)	510 kg (1125 lb)
4.0 mm (AWG 6)	905 kg (2000 lb)
5.0 mm (AWG 4)	1420 kg (3100 lb)

Breaking load of stainless wire, 7 x 7, 316 grade (guide only):

1.5 mm (AWG 15)	135 kg (300 lb)
2.0 mm (AWG 12)	240 kg (530 lb)
2.5 mm (AWG 10)	375 kg (825 lb)

Also available is micro-cable (suitable for light loads and less visible), which requires the use of micro-ferrules (see cable grips, fig. 1).

Breaking load of micro-cable:

0.26 mm (AWG 30)	6.5 kg (14 lb)
0.51 mm (AWG 24)	29 kg (64 lb)
1.0 mm (AWG 18)	60 kg (130 lb)

Wire should be cut cleanly with a pair of wire or cable cutters. Decent wire cutters are expensive, with Felco being probably the leading make. You may be able to cut thinner cable with some good-quality side cutters. Do not compromise: it is important that the cut is clean, to avoid fraying and also cutting yourself. It is not a bad idea to wrap the cut ends of cable with some insulating electrical tape.

To use the cable, you will have to attach it to various fittings. The best ones are made from stainless steel and are primarily for use on boats, so you will probably need to find a chandler (boat bits supplier) or buy online. Fittings come in a vast array of sorts and sizes; I have tried to cover the principles of the most common types. Some builders' merchants will stock an assortment of fittings; these are usually made from galvanised steel and tend to be cruder than their marine equivalents. They are, however, cheaper and thus aesthetically less refined, but they work in the same way as their posher cousins.

MAKING LOOPS

You will need to loop the cable in order to attach to hooks and eyes, etc. The loop is

MAKING LOOPS

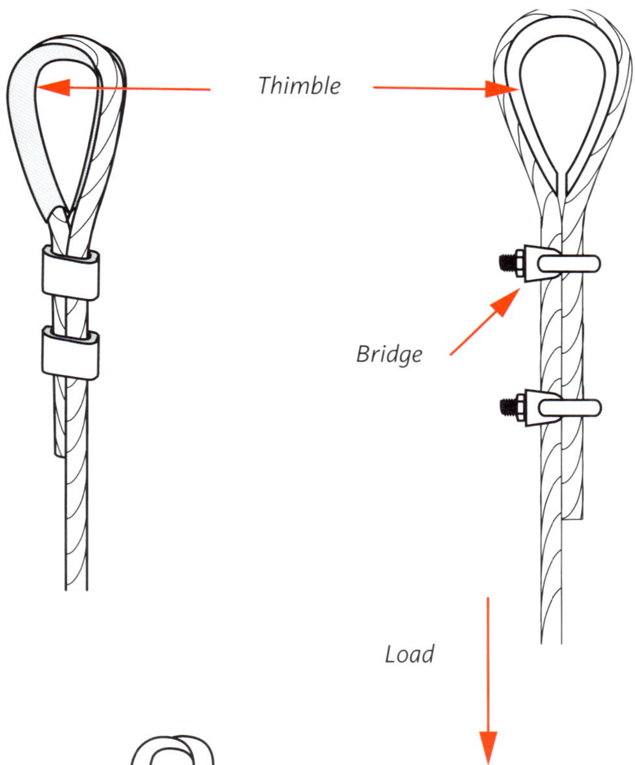

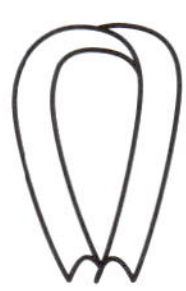

Thimble

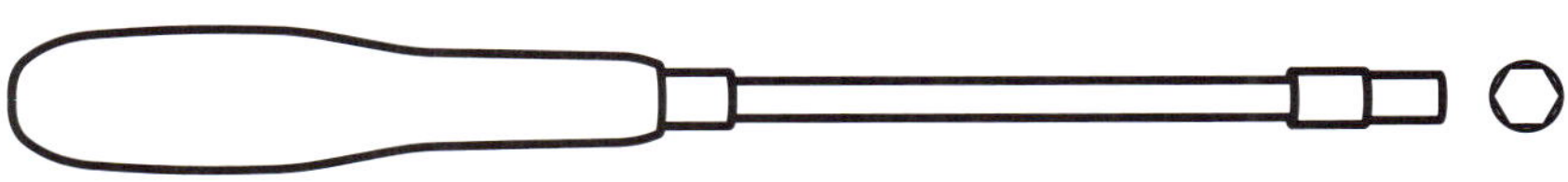

Nut spinner

formed by using a thimble and grips to secure the cable (see making loops diagrams). It's important to use a thimble, as this spreads the load across the cable.

CABLE GRIPS

You will need various tools, depending on the type of cable grip you use (see below). If you use crimps then a crimping tool is required. Barrel grips need a small or medium slotted screwdriver while duplex and U-shaped cable grips will need a small spanner or a nut spinner, the latter makes the job much easier and is well worth the investment if you're going to do a lot of this kind of work.

There are various cable grips on the market:

- Micro-ferrules, as the name suggests, are used with very thin wire, when hanging relatively light loads.

- Ferrules/crimps/swages are soft-metal barrels, either aluminium or copper, and need to be used with a crimping tool. This tool compresses the ferrule onto the wire; if you are working with very thin cable, you can use a pair of pliers and a vice to squash the crimp.

- Barrel grips are simple stainless-steel barrels with two screws that are tightened once the loop is made. They can also be used as stoppers along the length of the cable.

- Duplex grips consist of a channel with a plate that secures the cable using a couple of nuts. They are quite fiddly to thread, but they do look good.

CABLE GRIPS

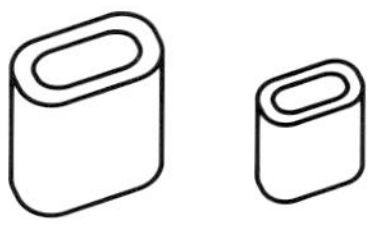

Crimps (ferrules)

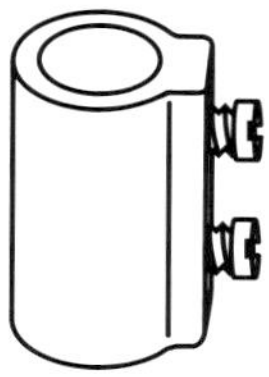

Barrel grip

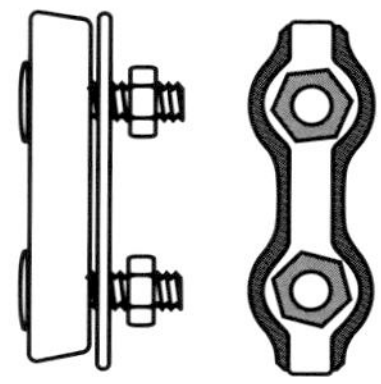

Duplex grip

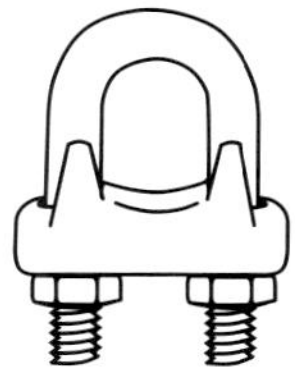

Cable grip

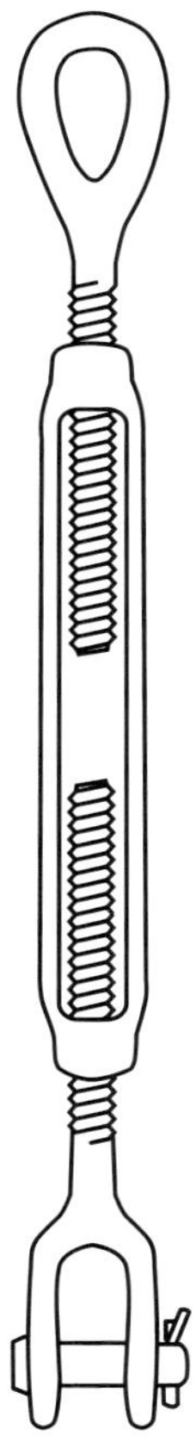

Straining screw (open type)

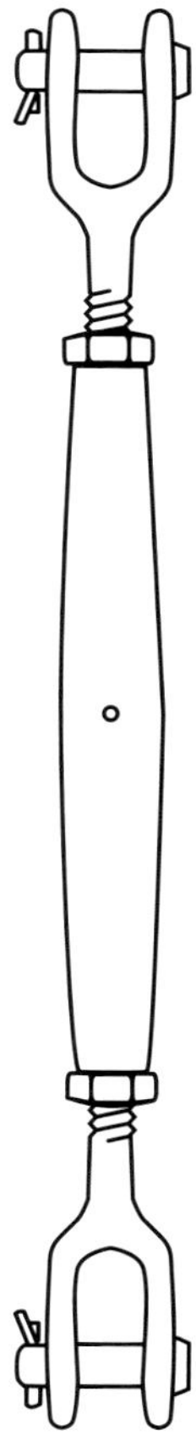

Straining screw (closed type)

Tightening of the nuts is best done with a nut spinner/driver or socket driver.

- Cable grips consist of a U-bolt and bridge, and once the cable is threaded they are tightened with two nuts. These are simple to use and very effective.

Make sure that the load-bearing part of the cable is against the bridge.

NB Always make sure that screws/nuts are tightened evenly, and I would recommend using two grips per loop. Use a nut spinner (fig. 4) or socket driver. Make sure you use the correct-size grips and thimble for the diameter of cable.

You can get loops made up professionally.

STRAINING SCREWS

Also known as bottle or rigging screws and turnbuckles.

When using cable with loops it's virtually impossible to get the cable to the exact length required, so straining screws are not only used for tensioning the cable, but also for making adjustments, and are particularly useful when hanging things like screens, which need to be level. They are available with both open and closed bodies and a variety of ends, eyes, hooks and forks (jaws) or combinations of these (see figs. 6 & 7).

FIXING

Unless the load is fairly light, it is normal to use Rawlbolts for solid ceilings or walls. If you're attaching to wooden beams, use eyebolts if you can; otherwise, pad eyes are good, providing they are securely fitted. If you're hanging a heavy load, always seek advice as to the strength of the ceiling you're fixing from: it may be that some sort of plate or structure is required to carry the load. It's also worth remembering that many galleries do not allow you to fix directly into the floor, so you will need to find some sort of compromise.

A variety of fixtures exist that can be attached to the work in order to attach a loop (see rigging accessories diagrams). These come in a multitude of sizes and forms; better-looking ones can be bought from a chandler, while the more basic types you'll find at builder's merchants and hardware stores.

Consider how they will be attached to the object, i.e. whether a screw(s) will suffice or whether a nut and bolt should be used. If you're making an object to be hung, think about making a hanging point as part of the work. You may be able to adapt 'off the shelf' fixtures for this, or you can buy specialist ones such as Bighead (see Useful websites, page 194) that can be bonded into your work.

For attaching things like frames, shelves or screens along the length of the cable, wire stoppers can be used. I've shown two types: a ball type and a two-part stopper that has the advantage of small teeth that grip the wire. Alternatively, a barrel grip could be used.

In practice it is often easier to assemble and hang the cable before attaching the work. In this case it is useful to use a shackle, or a carbine snap hook, as a link between the loop on the cable and the fixing on the object, to enable easy attachment and detachment.

NB If you're suspending work (see Working at heights), you're more than likely to be working at height, up ladders, etc., so always seek assistance and advice as necessary, and do not work alone.

When you are fixing from the ceiling, particularly if you have more than one suspension point, it is often easier to decide on the positioning of things on the floor. Points can be marked and transferred to the ceiling using a plumb line, which is basically a long length of string attached to a pointed weight. The end of the string is held against the ceiling and the plumb is dangled so that it almost touches the floor. The string is then manoeuvred across the ceiling until the plumb is directly over the mark on the floor; because it is hanging vertically, the mark can be replicated in the exact position on the ceiling. This will require assistance (see also Marking Out in AV Stage, page 132).

RIGGING ACCESSORIES

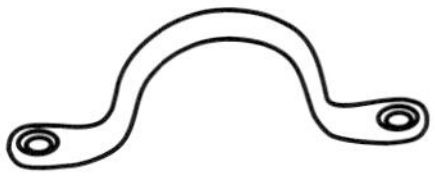

Eye strap

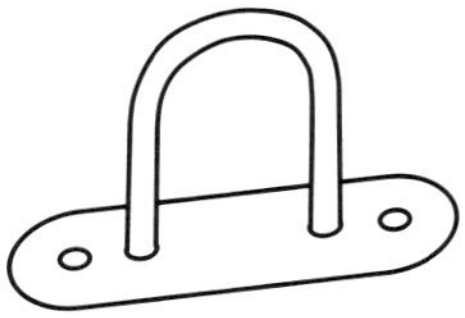

Pad eye

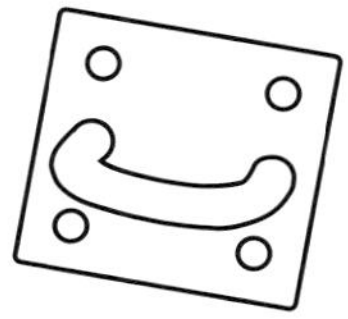

Eye plate

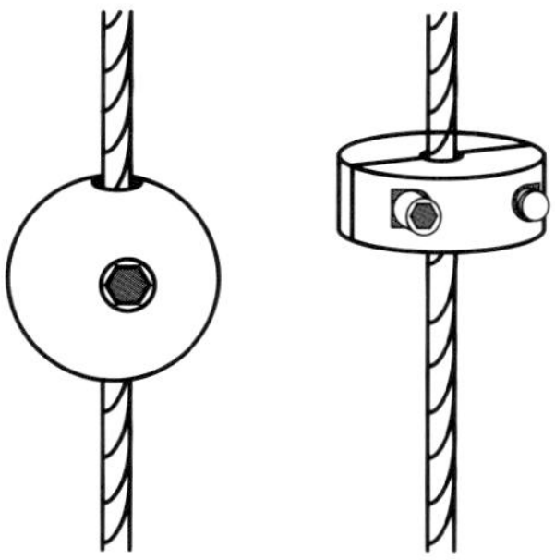

Wire stoppers

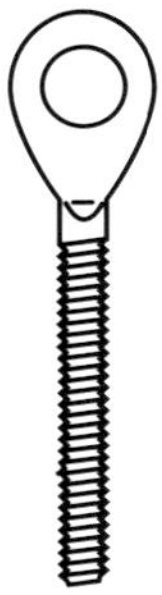

Thread eye

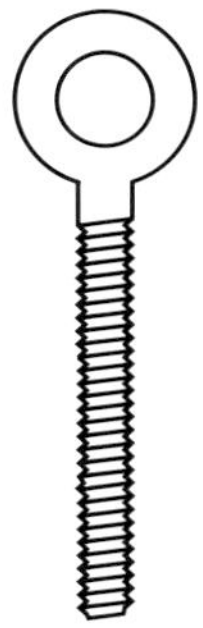

Eye bolt

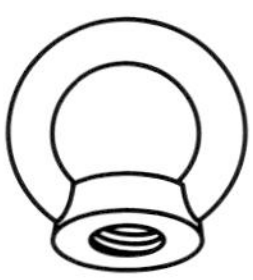

Eye nut

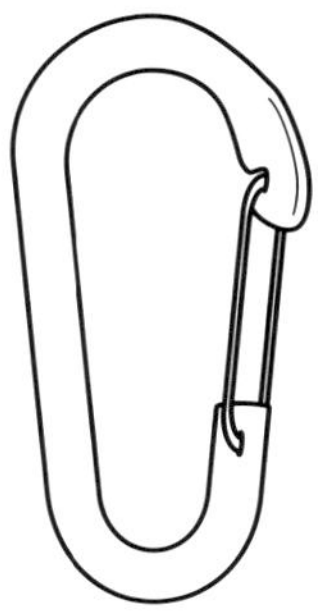

Carbine hook

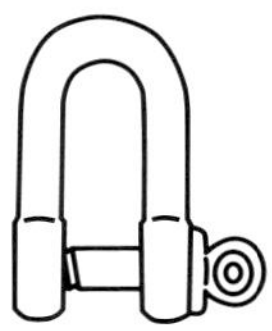

Shackle

RIGGING EXAMPLES

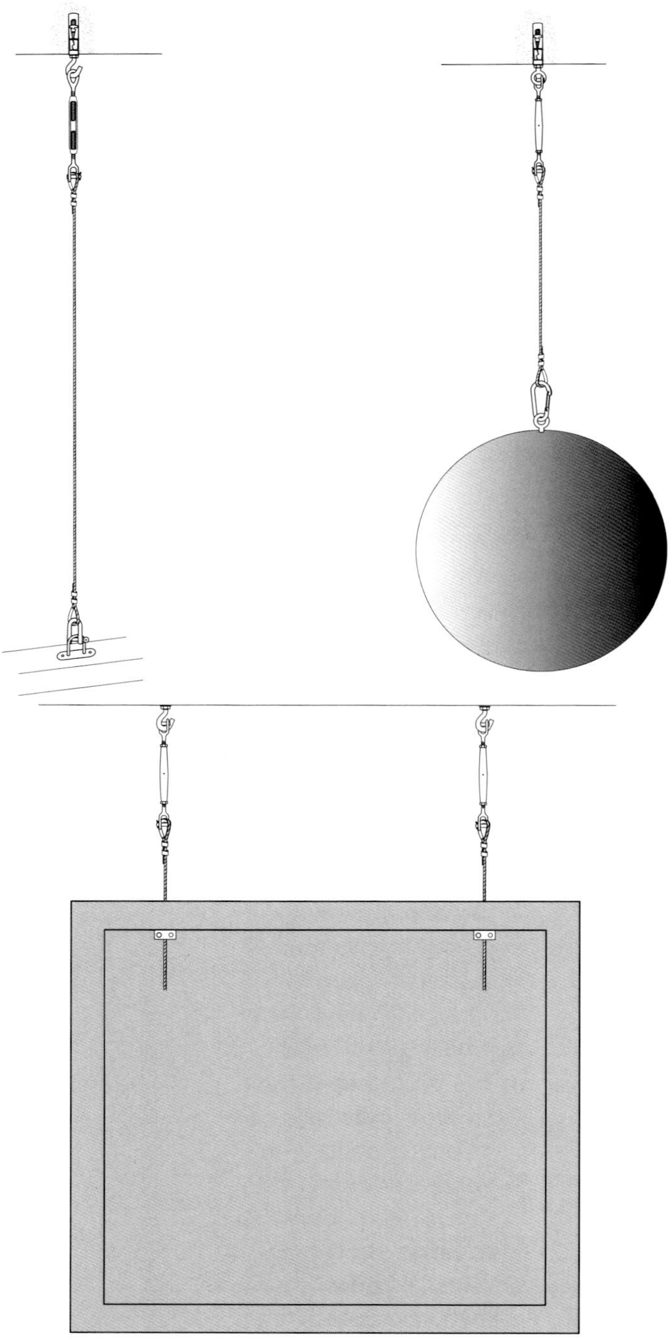

7

stage seven

AV

notes

AV

I'm sure you've been to exhibitions where videos aren't working. To try and avoid this, it is important to keep any AV installation as simple as possible: the fewer pieces of equipment, leads, etc. there are, the easier it will be both to set up and to keep running during the course of a show.

Keep the switching on and off as easy as possible and within reach. You should not need to go up ladders or into contortions in order to locate a piece of equipment.

Always provide clear, concise instructions that technicians, gallery managers or invigilators can understand. Remember that in large group exhibitions, such as BA or MA shows, there may be work by up to 50 people to turn on and keep running! Believe me, there is nothing worse than lying on your back in a space in which you can barely see anything, trying to read four sheets of badly written instructions. Which reminds me – a torch is a handy bit of equipment to have.

VIDEO

OK, you've shot and edited your video and will hopefully have decided how it will be shown, i.e. either projected or on a monitor. Remember that the installation of the work will have an effect on the viewer's perception of it, be it a straight cinematic projection or a complex installation. If you have an idea of how the piece will be shown before you start shooting/editing, so much the better; you don't want to fit a round peg into a square hole. As with any other work, see the installation as being part of the work and not some sort of afterthought.

DATA ADAPTORS

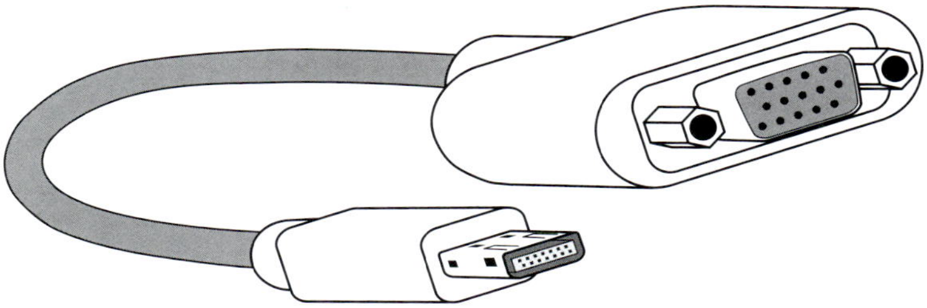

VGA to mini VGA

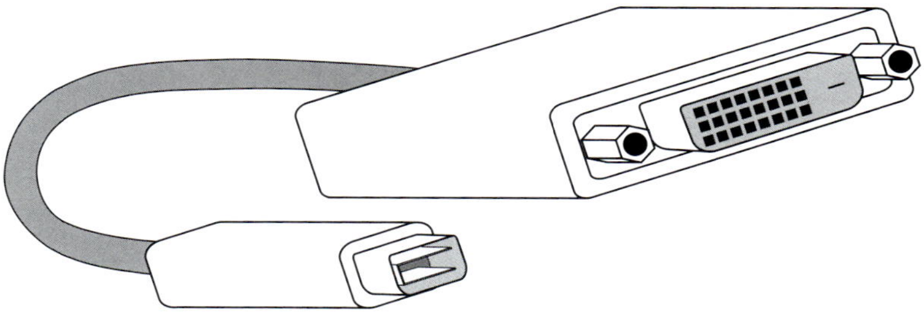

DVI to mini DVI

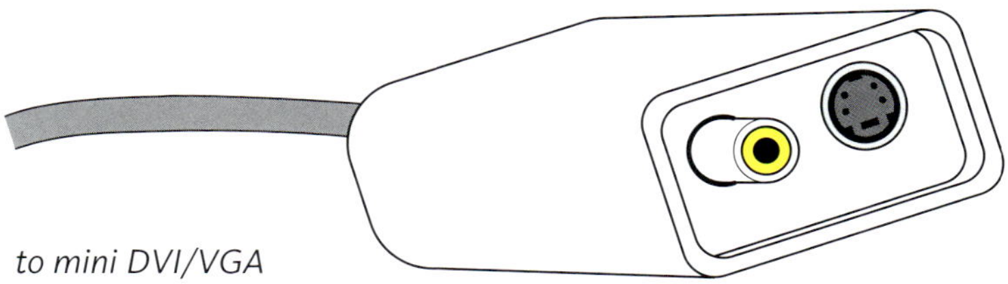

Phono/S video

VIDEO PROJECTORS

The quality of projectors has improved dramatically over the last few years. At the same time the cost has fallen considerably, so much so that it's now a realistic option to consider buying rather than renting, as you can always sell it on after the show.

If you are buying a projector, it is worth thinking about buying a spare bulb – these are expensive, but if you don't have a back-up, your show could be compromised. If this is not an option, then check the type of bulb and where you can purchase one from (most likely via the internet), and make sure there is an express-delivery option. If you are hiring, check out the replacement/insurance clause on the hire agreement, as you don't want to be lumbered with additional costs.

Projectors are now generally simple to set up and operate, unlike the older CRT type, with their three separate lenses that needed aligning and focusing. However, there are considerations you will need to think about before buying or renting:

- How dark is the space?
- What size is the intended image?
- What size is the space you are showing in?
- Check out the brightness of the projector. This is measured in lumens; the higher the number, the brighter the image.
- The lens. A ratio of 1:2 is common, i.e. you will get a 1 m (39 in.) wide image if the throw (the distance from projector to screen) is 2 m (78 in.). Some will have a zoom lens,

DATA LEADS

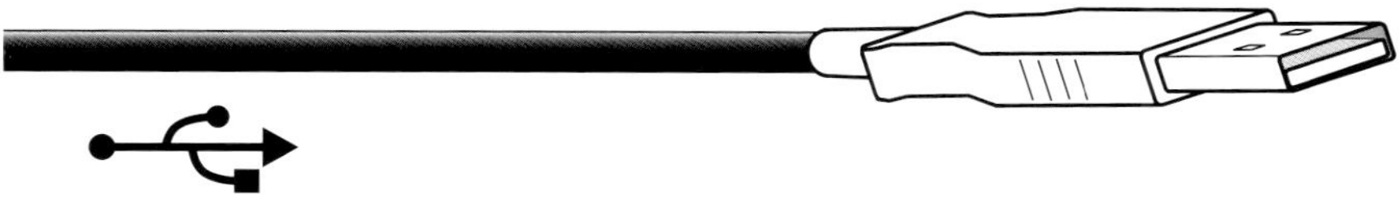

USB (A)

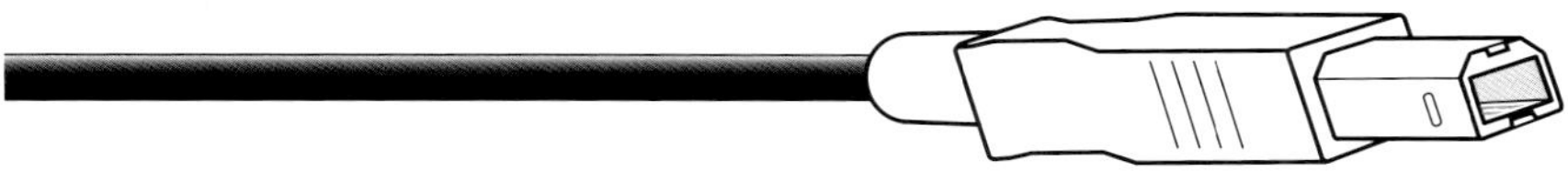

USB (B)

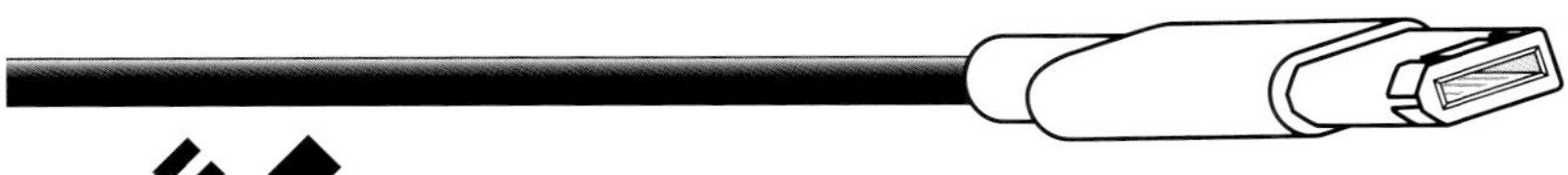

Firewire 6-pin

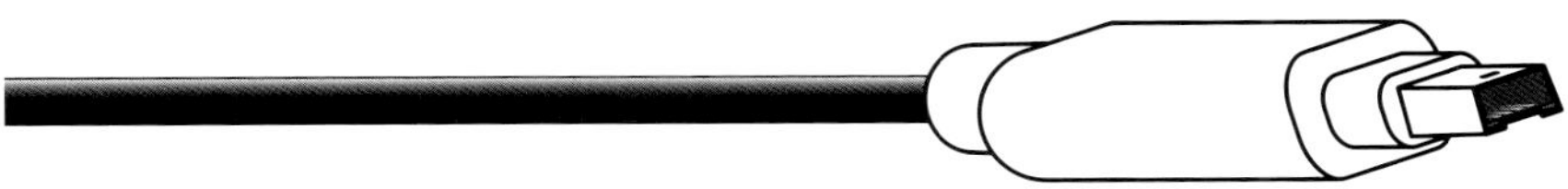

Firewire 4-pin

which typically gives 1:1.6 – 1:2.1. Wide-angle lenses are also an option, in some cases giving a 1:1 ratio.

- The resolution. How sharp will the image be? You will have probably seen video where the pixels are quite obvious, and some where the image is pin-sharp.

- The contrast ratio. This measures the blackest black to the whitest white; the greater the ratio, the greater the contrast given.

- Check out what inputs there are. It's unwise to buy a 'data only' projector. As well as a VGA input and possibly a DVI, it should have some video inputs, e.g. composite video, component video and s-video.

- Can you flip the image? This enables the projector to be hung upside down, which may be desirable in some set-ups.

- Does it have a keystone function? This will square the image when the projector is tilted at an angle to the screen, to avoid a trapezoid shape. However, you should be aware that there might be some loss of resolution if this function is used. Some projectors offer a lens shift as an alternative to keystoning, which avoids the above. Careful positioning of the projector and screen can sometimes avoid these problems.

- Aspect ratio. This is the relationship between the width and the height of the image. The conventional format is 4:3; widescreen is 16:9. What ratio is your video shot and edited at?

DATA LEADS

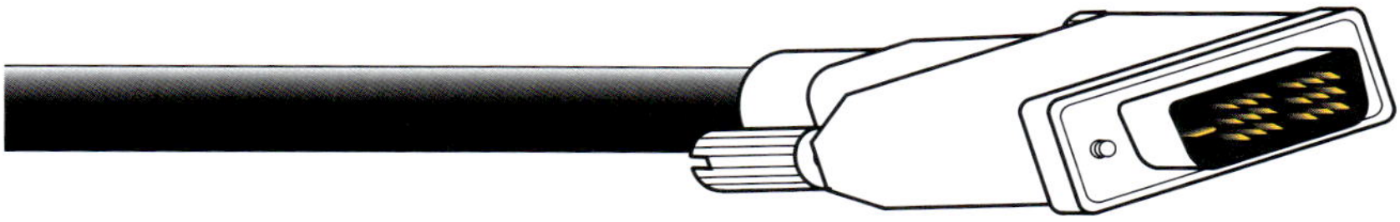

DVI

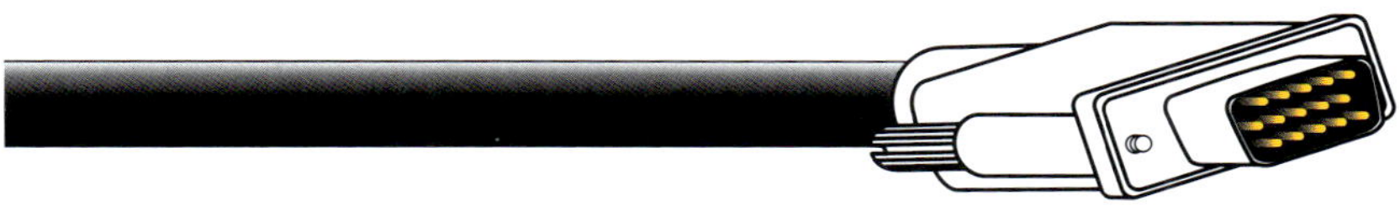

VGA

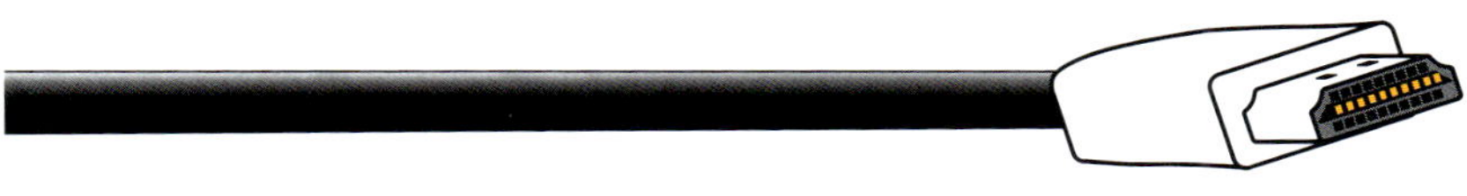

HDMI

- The better projectors use DLP or DMD technology, in which the image is made from the light being reflected off tiny mirrors.

All this information should be available from the manufacturer's website.

MONITORS

A monitor is used for displaying material from an external device to which it is directly linked, as opposed to a television, which has a tuner in order to pick up a signal from a remote transmitter.

We have entered the age of the flat screen; check out the brightness, the contrast ratio and the types of input. Also look at the refresh rate: the lower the number, the quicker the information is being changed on the screen. The viewing angles are also important: you don't want a screen that can only be viewed head-on.

Plasma screens are still very expensive and not always particularly good quality. CRT (cathode ray tube) monitors, although still available, are becoming a rarity. Consider how you want the installed video(s) to look.

Professional monitors will on the whole look better than domestic products. Do you want your installation to look like an extension of your living room?

PLAYING DEVICES

I think it safe to say that videotape recorders are now obsolete as a means of showing work. The most common method has become the DVD player, which is cheap, as well as easy to install and operate. Make sure when buying one that it is multi-regional, i.e. it plays burnt discs (- R if made with a Mac).

AUDIO-VISUAL LEADS

BNC (male)

BNC (female)

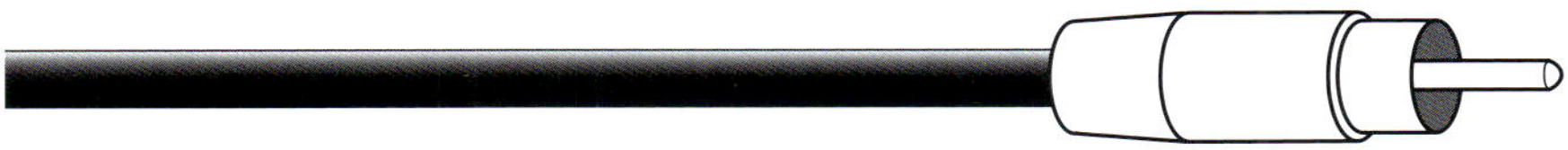

Phono (male)

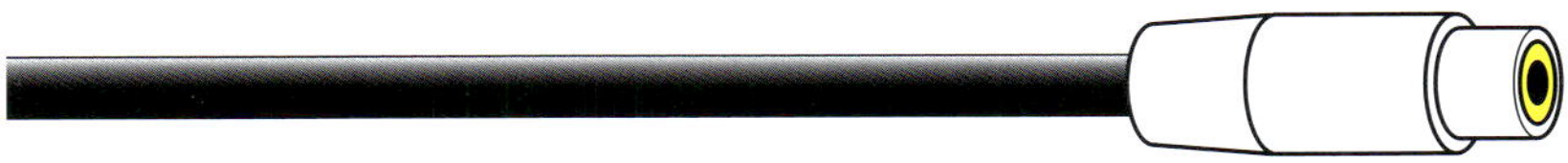

Phono (female)

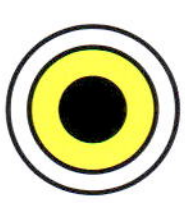

video

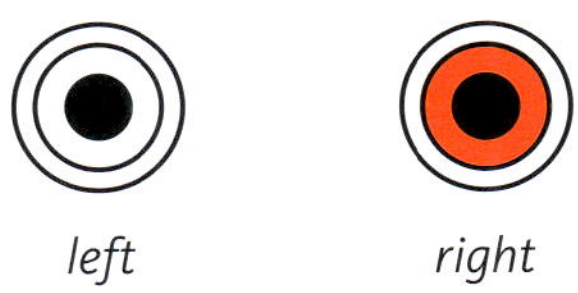

audio

Most DVD players are made to be operated horizontally. Take note that if they are wedged into plinths, etc. at an angle, it is more than likely that the disc will slide out, meaning no one will see your work. Think about where the player is, both in terms of ease of operating and aesthetics. Do not put it on top of a projector: if a DVD gets hot it won't work. You can always run a long cable from the DVD to the monitor or projector.

NB Always have a back-up disc.

For multi-screened work DVD players can be synched. You will, however, need to hire professional-quality players and a synch unit, and the work will need to be edited accordingly.

High Definition video formats and equipment, together with Blu-ray and its alternative HD-DVD disc players, are all on the market. Whilst still expensive, the cost of these is bound to come down. It is still not clear which format, Blu-ray or HD-DVD, will win out, or indeed be overtaken by another format.

Computers are being used more frequently as input devices; items like a Mac mini are small and unobtrusive. The information can be stored directly on the hard disk, and the program launched when the computer is turned on.

PROJECTION

Preparation

Before starting you will need to work out the size of the image and the distance from the

AUDIOVISUAL LEADS

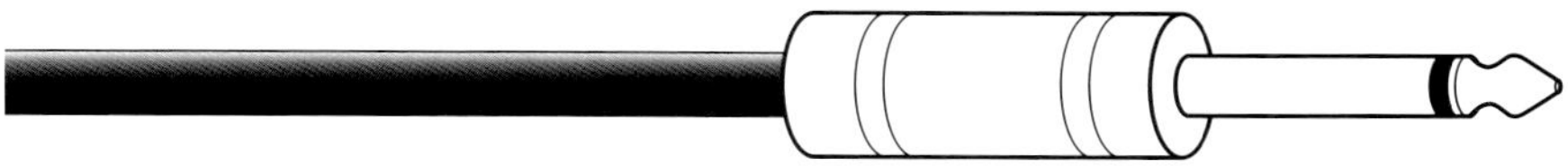

6.25 mm (1/4 in.) mono jack plug

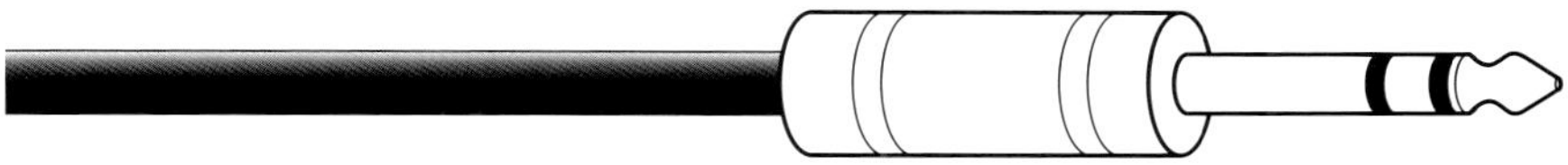

6.25 mm (1/4 in.) stereo jack plug

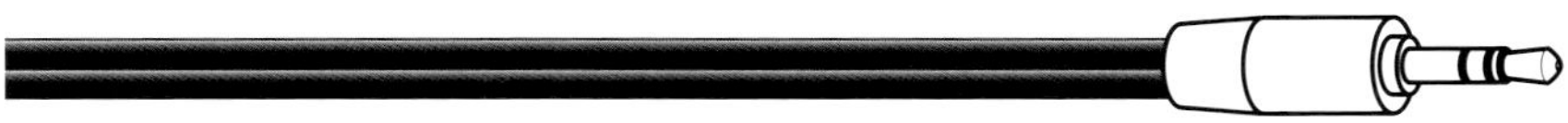

3.5 mm (1/2 in.) stereo mini jack plug

projector to the screen, taking note the constraints of the space you are showing in (fig. 1). If you don't have the projector to hand, you should be able to check out the throw on the manufacturer's website, and there's also a useful website for working out the relative distances, www.projectorcentral.com/projection-calculator-pro.cfm

Suspending video projectors

It may not always be possible to put video projectors on a wall-mounted shelf or desirable to have them on top of a plinth. The following section gives instructions for a relatively easy hanging system, which is both very stable and easily adjustable.

Also worth remembering is that most projectors have an offset beam (fig. 2), so it may be worth having the projector hanging upside down. Make sure the projector can flip the image, otherwise you will have to do this in post-production. Being upside down means that the projector can be hung higher, i.e. above head height, and the shelf can be level or sloping as desired.

Most projectors have three threaded locating holes on the base. Make a paper pattern of these by simply laying a piece of paper on the base, lining up the front edge and stabbing through with a pencil where the holes are. These marks can then be transferred to your shelf. You will need to buy some longish bolts and some nuts/washers (50–60 mm/2–2½ in.) to fit. Projectors usually take M4 or M3 thread size, but this may vary. Bolting the projector to the shelf also offers security, and is worth considering if the projector is on top of the shelf, or when using plinths and a wall-mounted unit. It also has the advantage of

PROJECTION

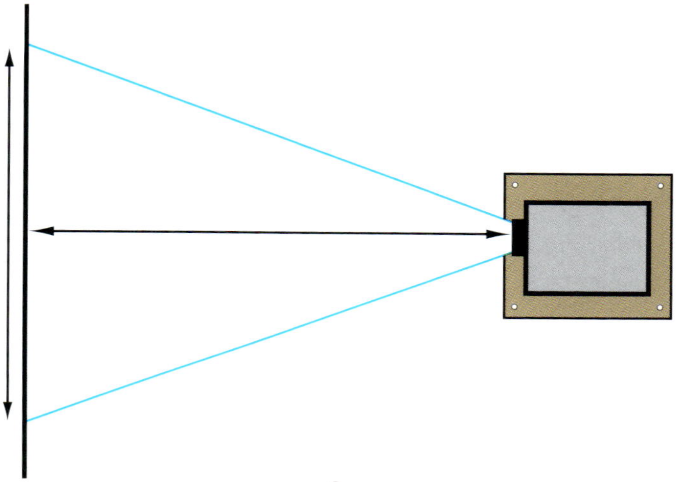

fig. 1

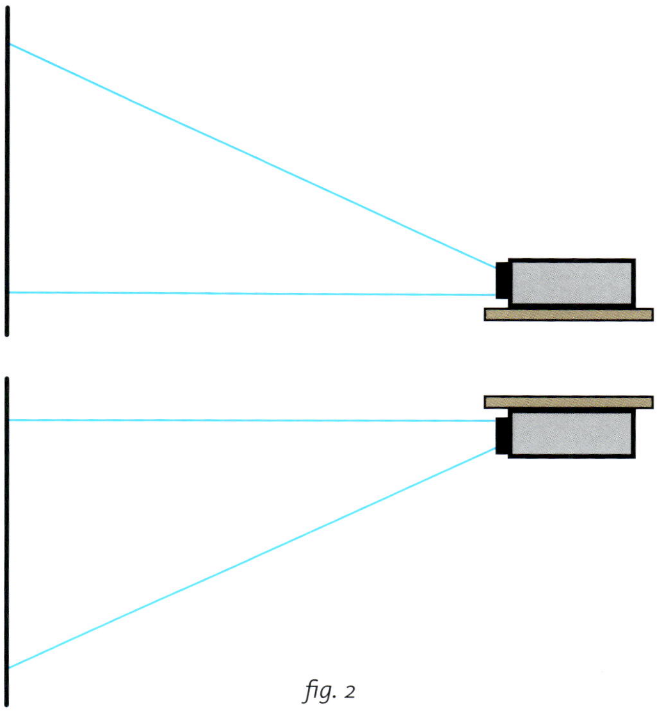

fig. 2

giving a degree of adjustability.

You will need shelves, 4 x lengths of studding, 4 x nuts, bolts and washers, plus 4 x nuts, bolts & washers per additional shelf and 4 x Rawlbolts (loose type).

Make shelves for the projector and any other items required to go with it, e.g. a DVD player, amp, speakers. Make sure they are large enough to accommodate the equipment, allowing for leads and also room in the corners to put holes for the studding; these need to be at least 25 mm (1 in.) in from the edges. Drill these holes slightly larger than the size of the studding you are using. Projectors should always have their own shelf, as they give off a lot of heat.

Marking out

Place the projector on top of the shelf on the floor, at the distance you have previously worked out. Make sure that the front edge is parallel to the screen or wall that you are planning to project onto.

Mark out the position of the shelf on the floor, through the corner holes (fig. 3).

Using a plumb line, transfer these marks onto the ceiling. You'll need a helping hand with this: one person up the ladder placing the line and marking, the other on the floor, checking that the plumb is dropping vertically onto the correct position, and giving instructions ('left a bit, right a bit', etc.). (fig. 4).

MARKING OUT

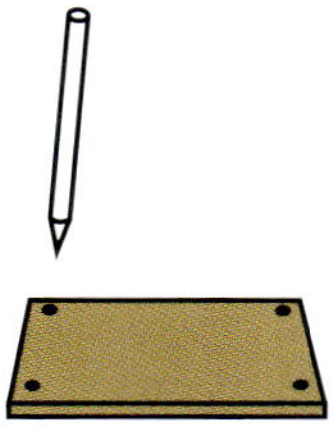

fig. 3

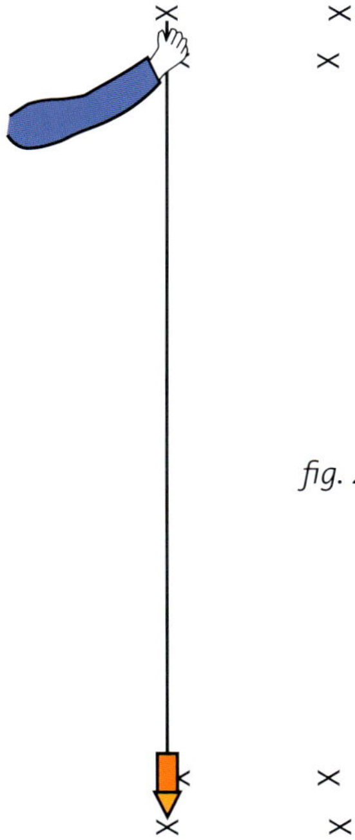

fig. 4

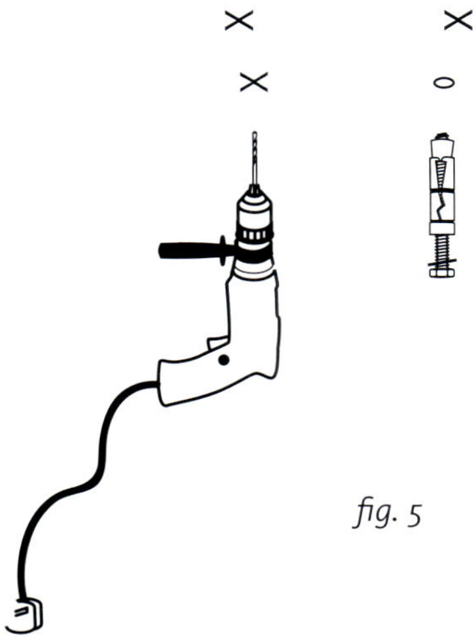

fig. 5

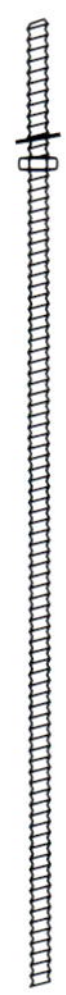

studding

Fixing

Drill the holes for the Rawlbolt fixings (fig. 5) – M6 or M8 should suffice (see page 70).

Put the Rawlbolts in place and set. You can either put in the 'loose bolt' type and set with the bolt provided, or use the studding with nut and washer and set in the same way. If using the loose bolt type, remove the bolt and replace with the studding, washer and nut (fig. 6).

Once all four lengths of studding are secured, the shelves can be added using the washers/nuts on the underside of the shelf. It's probably easier to fix the projector to the shelf before attaching the shelf to studding (fig.7).

Level the front of the projector shelf using a spirit level. Test the projector for throw, and adjust the rear nuts up or down accordingly. Level any other shelves (fig. 8).

PLINTHS, SHELVES AND RIGGING

Of course this is not the only way of placing a projector. Figs 9, 10 and 11 show a rigged suspension, shelf and plinth (see the relevant stages for more information).

It's worth noting that slide projectors need a sturdy structure as they vibrate with the changing of the slides, therefore using the wire-rigging alternative is not recommended. Also, with film projectors it's best to stick to a solid plinth; ease of access is vital, and they are not items you can switch on and forget.

FILM PROJECTION

16 or 35 mm film offers a high-quality, distinctive feel; 16 mm is the format most commonly used by artists, unless they have a high budget.

FIXING

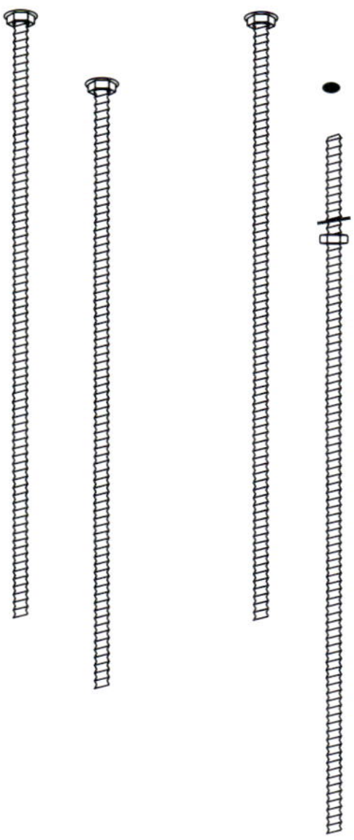

fig. 6

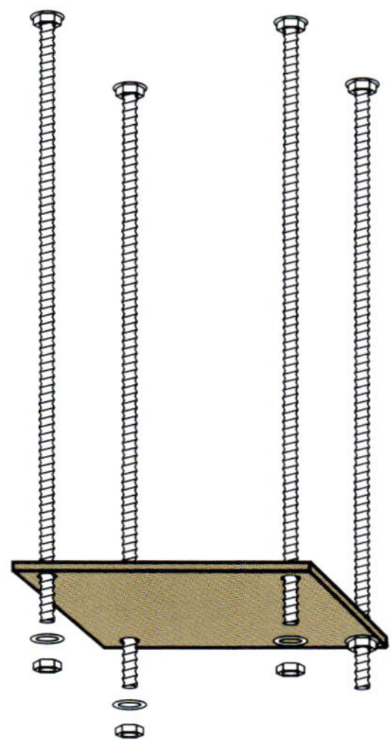

fig. 7

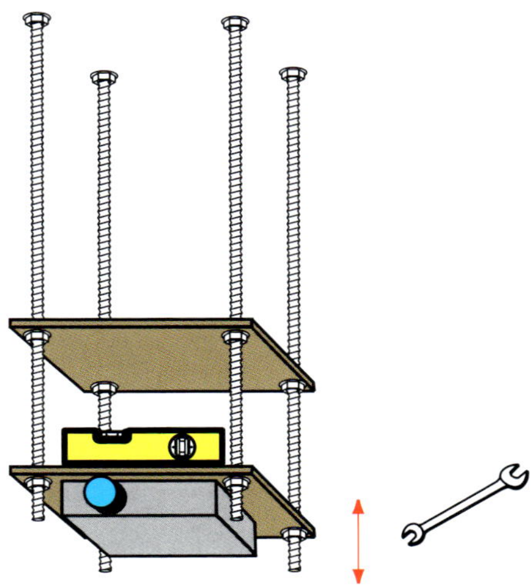

fig. 8

Because of the nature of the material, film is vulnerable and is thus usually only shown in screenings. However, it is possible to loop film so that it repeats; this can be done by simply making the film into a loop of the required duration, and hanging it above the projector on a series of hoops to keep the correct tension. Alternatively (and safer), you can hire specialist looping devices that attach to the top of the projector.

Remember that repeated playing of the film will result in wear and tear on both the image and the sprocket holes. Also, projectors do overheat, particularly in confined spaces. So if you are planning to use film, seek professional advice. The other alternative is to shoot in film and then transfer the footage to video.

SLIDE PROJECTION

Slide projectors are slowly disappearing, but they do offer a high-quality image. If just one image is being projected, always have several back-up slides to hand, as slides do fade quite rapidly when constantly projected.

Simple timing devices are available which plug into the back of the projector for multiple slides. Make sure all 80 spaces in a carousel are filled; to achieve this, you may need to copy and repeat your sequence.

If you are using more than one projector in a slide sequence, you can operate them via a computer program or tape/slide device, which enables them to be synched.

NB Always have a back-up copy of slides.

PROJECTION

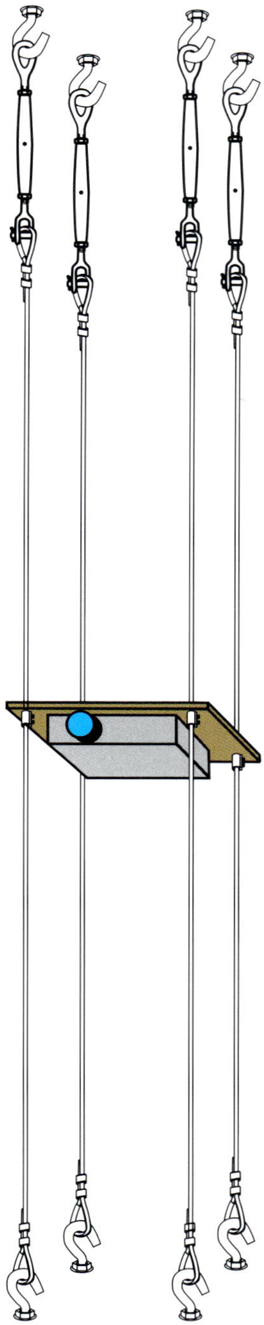

fig. 9

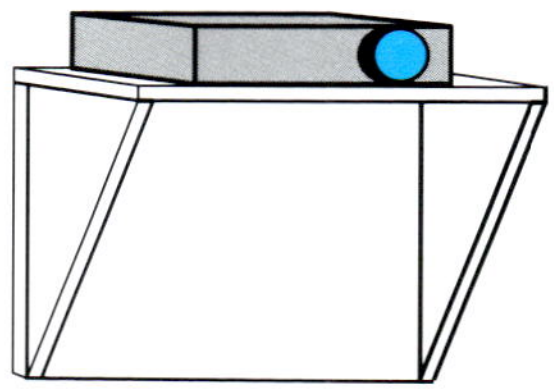

fig. 10

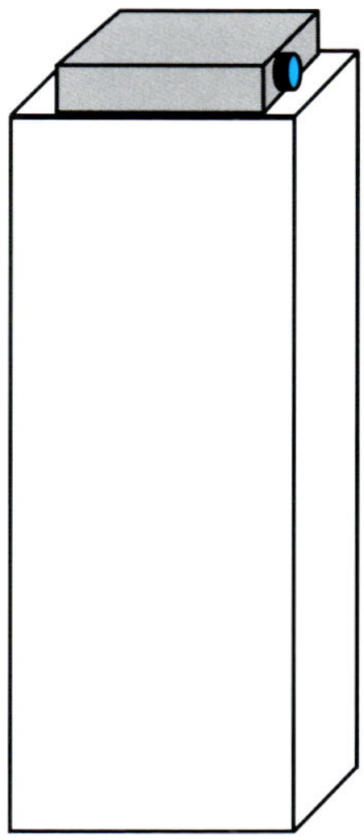

fig. 11

SCREENS

When you're looking at video or projected work in galleries, take note as to how it is screened.

Simple projections are made directly onto a wall. However, if the wall is not suitable you may need to construct a screen, to hang either on the wall or within the space. There is also the possibility of back projection, where the projector is behind the screen and the viewer in front, thereby eliminating the possibility of intrusion, as in fig. 1 (Back Projection). Remember, you will need more space to do this. Mirrors can be used in restricted spaces, but this requires both experience and time – it is not easy!

Screens can be made from sheet material like MDF, which has a nice smooth surface. The big drawbacks with this are its size and its weight; remember that the standard size of sheet wood is 2440 x 1220 mm (96 x 48 in.), so if a large screen is needed, then it will have to be joined. It will also require painting.

Foamex board, which has a Mylar surface and a matt white finish (no painting), is fairly light and works very well.

There are several specific screen materials on the market: one is a material covered in tiny glass beads, which is claimed to increase both the brightness and the vibrancy of the image.

Back-projection material (vinyl) works equally well for front projection, and is sold by the metre (yard). I've generally found the grey variety works best, but you can also get it in white.

It's usual to stretch the material over a frame, to avoid any rippling. This is done in pretty

BACK PROJECTION

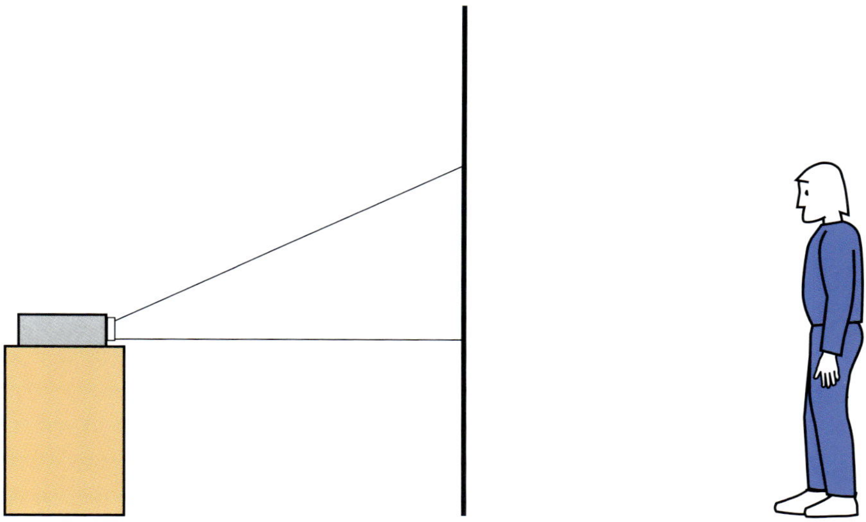

fig. 1

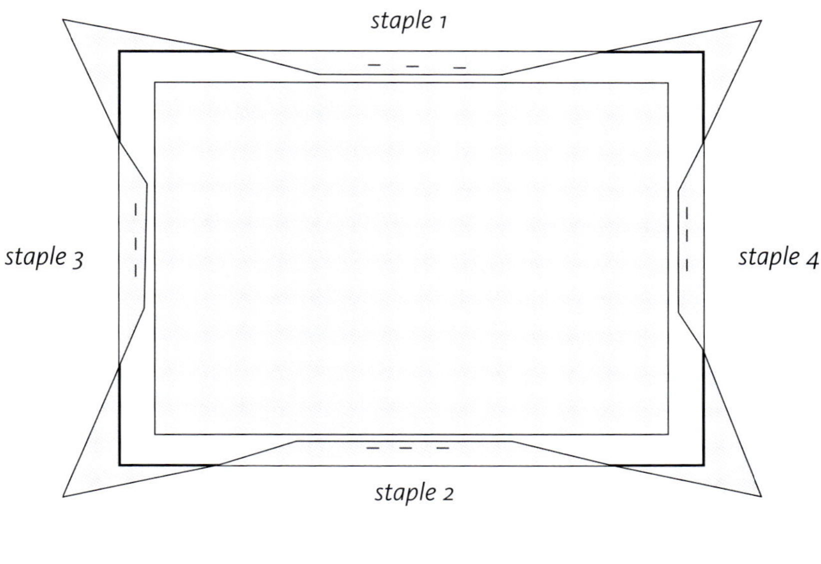

fig. 2

much the same way as a painter would stretch a canvas, i.e. working from the centre to the corners, keeping an even tension by working around the frame, fig. 2. Stapling the material is fine, but I would recommend reinforcing with gaffer tape, which both stops any likelihood of accidental tearing and makes staple removal easier afterwards, so that you can reuse the material.

Materials like tracing paper, gauzy linens, cotton and polythene sheets, and opaque Perspex (Plexiglas) can all be used – it really depends on the intention of the work and the installation.

Getting your projection angle and screen set up does take time. At the end of the day it's how your work is seen that matters, so don't leave it to the last minute!

AUDIO

CD/DVD, MiniDisc and MP3 players are all easy to use and install (most will have a repeat mode). DVD is particularly good, as you can burn it so as to repeat.

Check sound levels and the bleed into other spaces. You may have to do some negotiating on this front, so be realistic, and if necessary either bring the noise level down or think of time slots. Alternatively, you may want to provide earphones, though this obviously has a bearing on how the work is seen.

Check out that the space is suitable; in some places the sound booms or echoes so much that listening can be impossible.

8

stage eight

basic construction

notes

MAKING A PLINTH

First of all decide on the dimensions of the plinth. Remember that sheet wood, MDF, plywood, blockboard and chipboard are all sold in a standard size, 2240 x 1220 mm (96 x 48 in.), commonly referred to as an 8 x 4; so try and work within this size (fig. 1).

Generally, I would recommend using 12 mm (½ in.) MDF, which cuts cleanly and has a smooth finish if you want to paint it.

Make a cutting list. You will need four sides and a top. Let's say you are making a plinth 1000 mm (39 in.) high, 400 mm (16 in.) wide and 400 mm (16 in.) deep, from 12 mm (½ in.) MDF. The cutting list for this size will be (fig. 2):

2 x 988 x 400 mm (2 x 38½ x 16 in.)	sides a. and b.
2 x 988 x 376 mm (2 x 38½ x 15 in.)	sides c. and d.
1 x 400 x 400mm (1 x 16 x 16 in.)	top

The height of the sides is 988 mm (38 ½ in.); this allows for the thickness of the top, cut from 12 mm (½ in.) MDF sheet.

The width of sides c. and d. is 376 mm (15 in.), which is 400 – 24 mm (2 x 12 mm) or 16 – 1 in. (2 x ½ in.). This allows for the overlap (fig. 3).

It's not worth drawing everything out on the sheet of MDF, because when you cut it you will lose 2 to 3 mm (up to ⅛ in.) in each cut, so mark as you go (some saws will have built-in measuring devices). Nevertheless, think about

MAKING A PLINTH

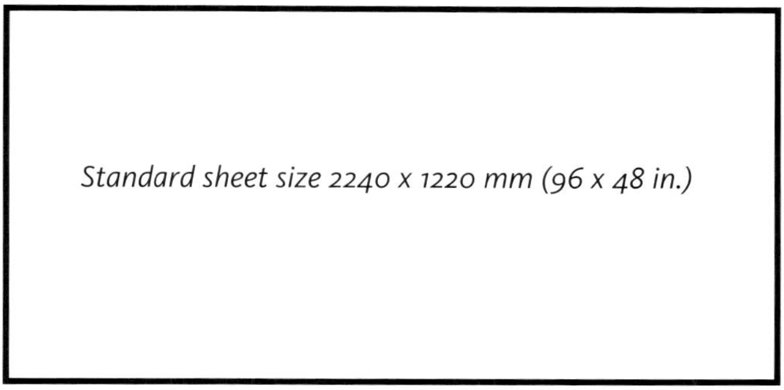

fig. 1

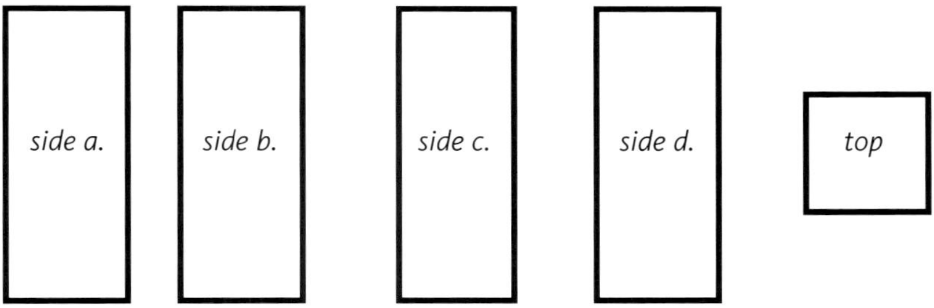

fig. 2

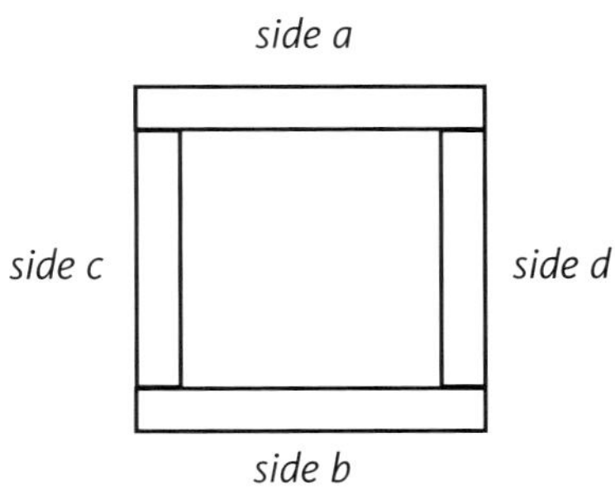

fig. 3

NB Not to scale

the most economical way of cutting the pieces from the sheet. If you can, get the board cut on a table saw.

Once you have got the pieces cut, it is then time to put them together. Ideally, this is best done using a vice on a workbench. However, if the plinth is to be made in the space, portable, foldable, cheap workbenches such as the Black & Decker Workmate are really good.

I recommend using screws rather than nails. If the plinth is going to hold particularly heavy weights or be stressed in any way, e.g. being used to sit/stand on, then use glue; otherwise, it is optional. If you don't glue it, you have the option of taking the plinth apart at the end of the show and flat-packing it.

- Pre-drill and countersink sides a. and b. (fig. 4) at approximately 200–250 mm (8–10 in.) apart. Make sure that the drill is held vertically and the holes are 6 mm (¼ in.) in from the edge; you may want to mark this before drilling (fig. 5).

NB Always make sure that the holes at the corners are at least 60 mm (2½ in.) along, otherwise you run the risk of the board splitting. Use a countersink to ensure the screws sink below the surface – you can get bits that will drill and countersink at the same time (see Basic Tools section, page 13).

- Take side c. and place firmly in the vice, spreading the glue along the top edge if needed (fig. 6).

MAKING A PLINTH

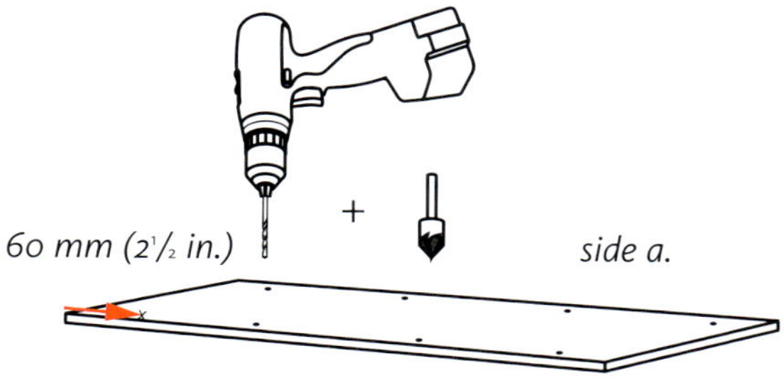

fig. 4

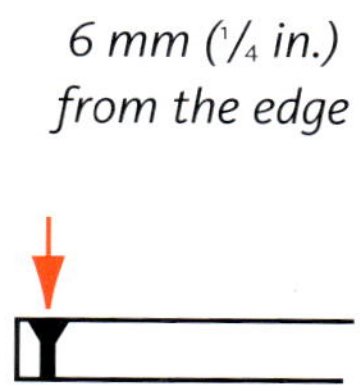

fig. 5

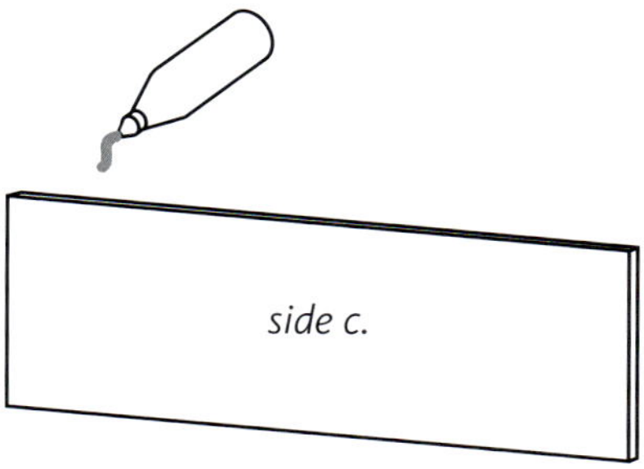

fig. 6

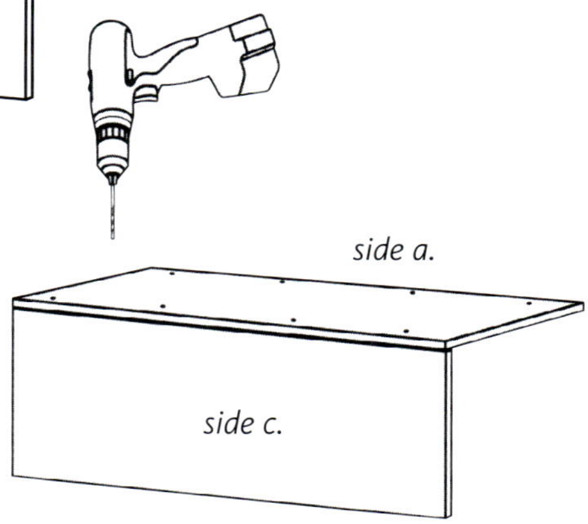

fig. 7

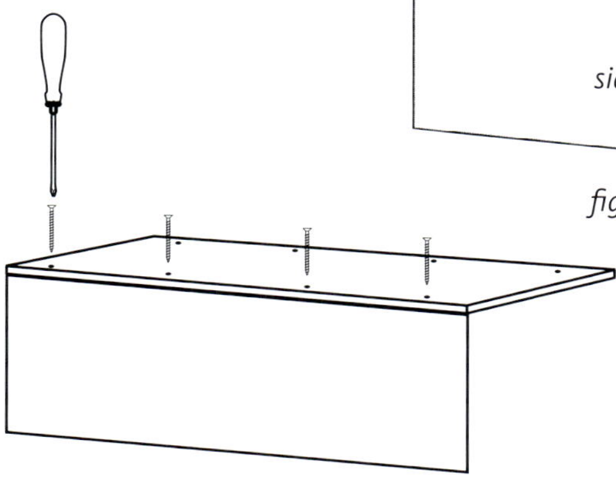

fig. 8

- Take side a. and place along the edge of side c.
- Make sure that the ends butt up to each other, and the edge of side a. is lined up with the edge of side c. (fig. 7). Drill into side c. through the pre-drilled holes in side a.
- Screw in the countersunk screws, using 4 x 35–40 mm (8 x 1³⁄₈ –1⁵⁄₈ in.) (see fig. 8).

NB To position the two sides accurately, you may find it easier to drill and screw the first hole, before commencing with the rest.

- Take side d., position, glue, drill through and screw as before (fig. 9).
- Take side b., position, glue, drill through and screw as before (fig.10).
- Pre-drill and countersink the top. I recommend at least two screws per side, remembering not to put holes too near the corners (fig. 11).
- Stand the four sides upright and position one edge of the top, then glue, drill through and screw (fig. 12).

NB If you're using glue, run it around all the sides before adding the top.

- If the sides are not quite square, adjust them by pulling in or out so that they align with the top, then drill through and screw the

MAKING A PLINTH

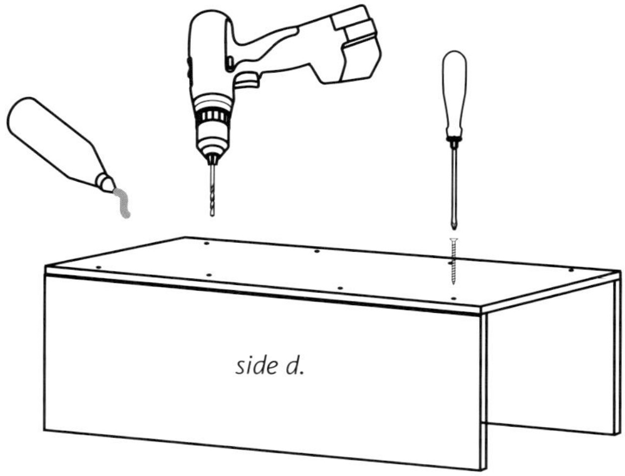

fig. 9

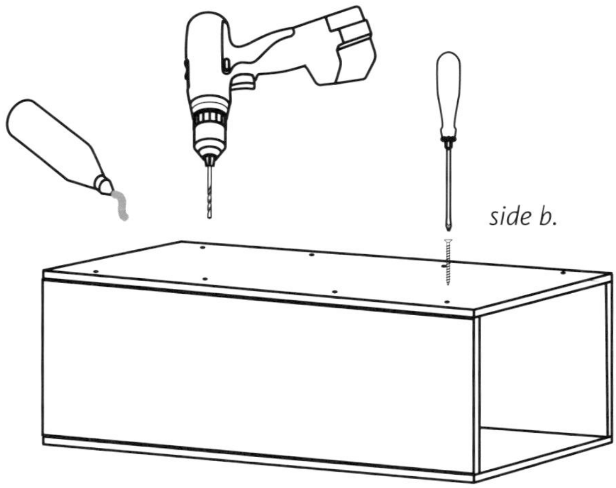

fig. 10

remaining sides (fig. 13).

- Finally, finish as needed: fill over the screw heads and paint using a roller rather than a brush.

This simple method of making can be applied to a wide range of constructions.

MAKING A PLINTH

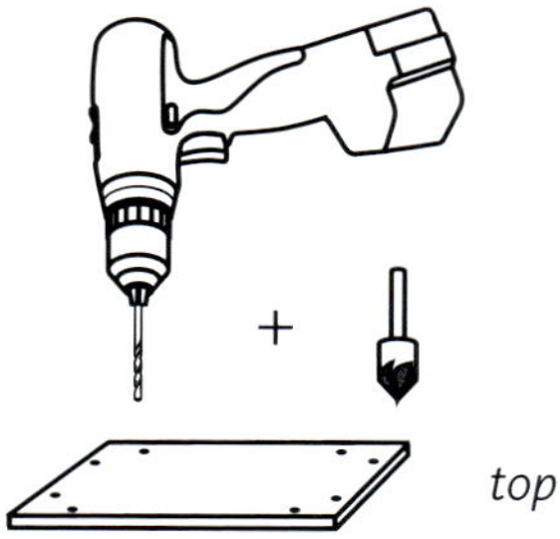

fig. 11

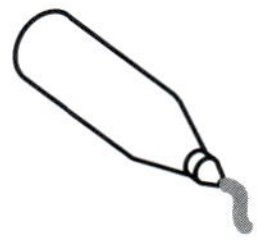

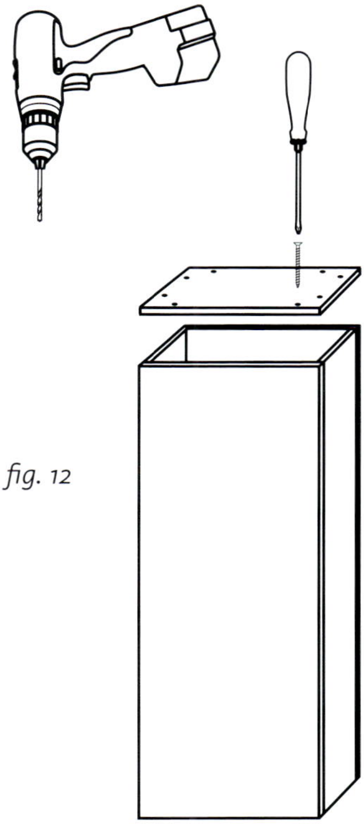

fig. 12

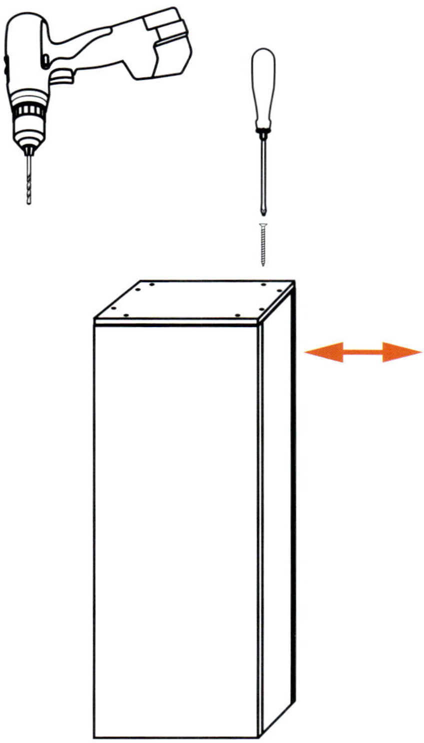

fig. 13

ADAPTING PLINTHS

The plinths can easily be adapted to house DVD players and the like, with the addition of shelves, hatches or a base; so if you were making a base or shelf for the above, the size would be 376 x 376 mm (15 x 15 in.), i.e. 24 mm (2 in.) less than 400 x 400 mm (16 x 16 in.), to allow for the thickness of the MDF (see the diagrams on adapting plinths).

Plinths are also used in conjunction with Perspex (Plexiglas) tops for showing items that are either valuable or delicate, or maybe for aesthetic reasons. I would advise having them made professionally, before you make the plinth. It is obviously easier to make the plinth to suit the Perspex, rather than the other way round. It will also look better if the Perspex top is inlaid into the plinth. A shallow inner piece is added to the top, in order to create a lip that the Perspex box can be dropped onto. This will also ensure the cover is stable.

NB When getting things like Perspex covers made professionally, remember to allow time for this.

ADAPTING PLINTHS

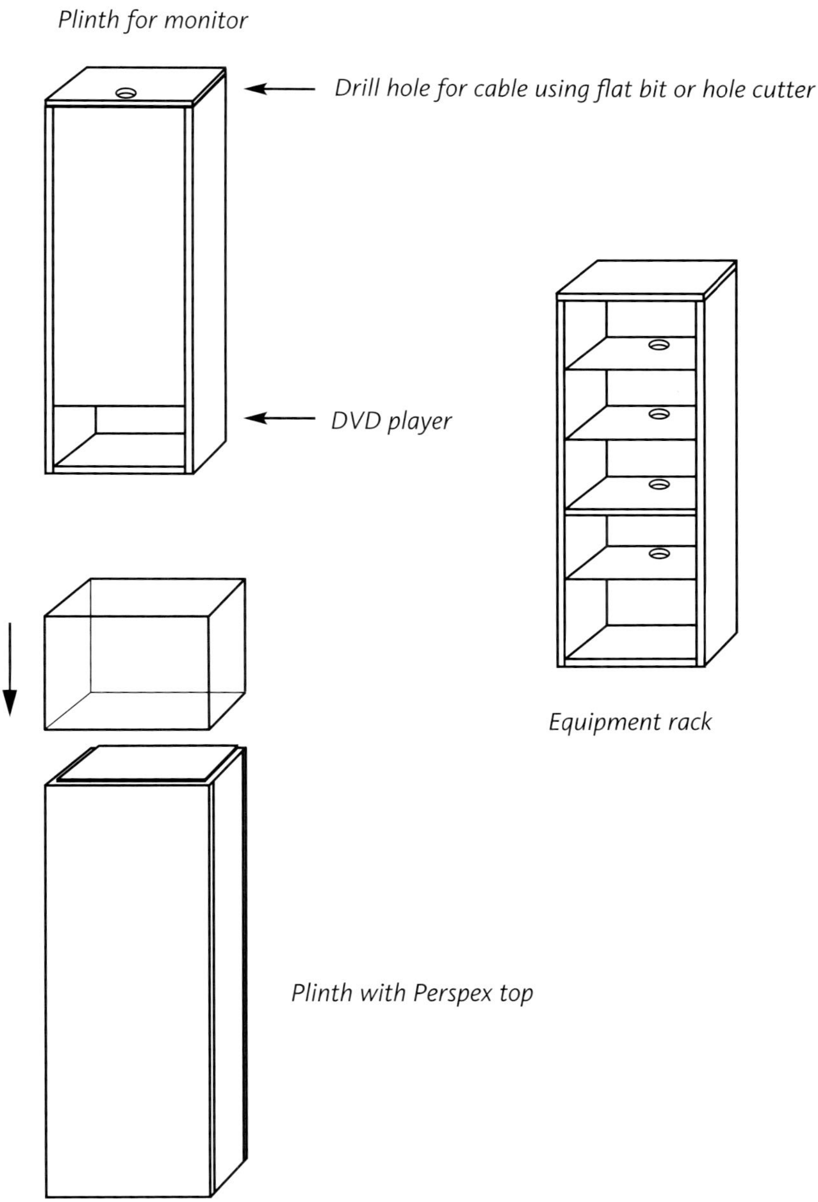

FLAT-PACKS

As I mentioned before, it is possible to make the plinth in flat-pack form, enabling it to be used several times.

The simplest solution is to make it as in Making a Plinth, without the addition of glue, so that they can simply be unscrewed and packed. It's probably worth considering using 15 or 18 mm (5/8 or 3/4 in.) MDF rather than the 12 mm (1/2 in.), as this will increase the durability. As the screws are going to need removing, the heads should remain visible; and as you will not be able to fill over them, so it is worth paying more attention to the spacing of the screws, i.e. to make sure they are the same distances apart on all the sides.

If you're intending to disassemble the plinth, it's likely that eventually the screws will lose their bite, so consider using different methods of fastening. Two examples are shown below.

CROSS-DOWEL BOLTS AND CROSS DOWELS

This method uses two pieces of ironmongery to fasten the boards together. As the bolt and dowel are placed in pre-drilled holes, there is less likelihood of degrading; they can also look a bit more attractive and intended than screws. A fair degree of accuracy is also needed. The bolts can be bought in various lengths and have a hex/Allen-key head. The dowels have a slotted head and can be bought either with a flange or without. It's easier to use the ones without, as they do give a bit more play; the flange type relies on very accurate drilling, as the flange sits on the outer surface.

FLAT-PACKS

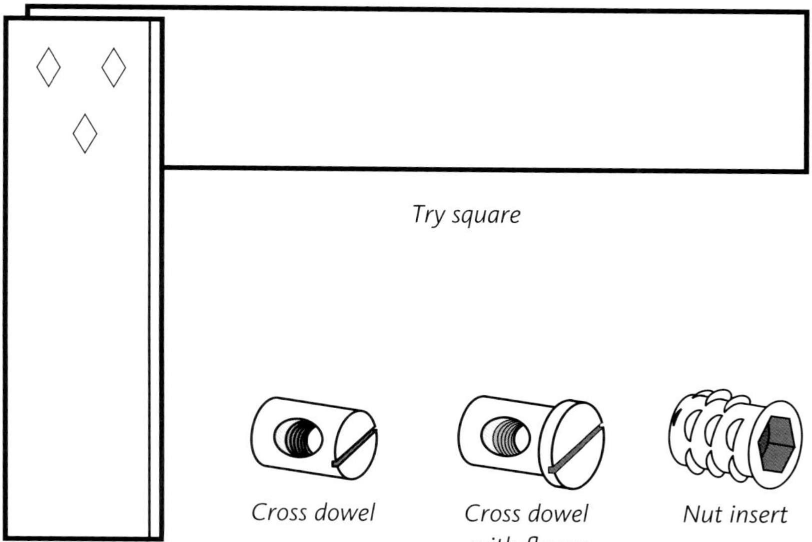

Try square

Cross dowel

Cross dowel with flange

Nut insert

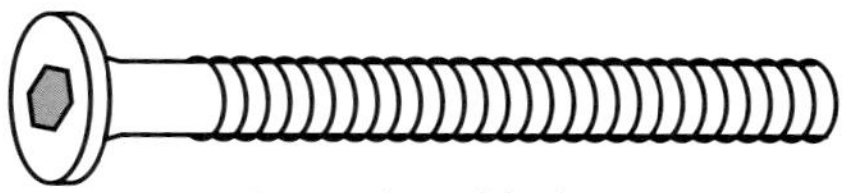

Cross-dowel bolt

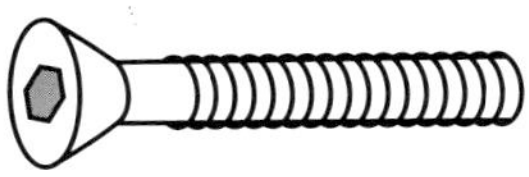

Countersunk bolt

Hex/Allen key

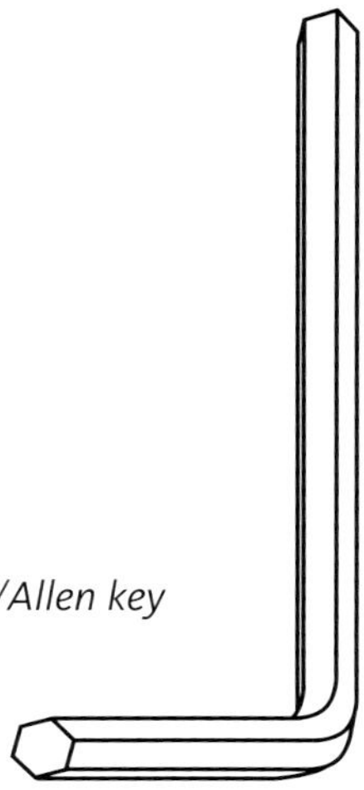

You will need a try square for setting out and a tape measure/rule, a slotted screwdriver and the appropriate hex/Allen key for the bolt. A marking gauge will also be useful if you know how to use one.

- Once the sides are cut to size, mark out as in fig. 1; make sure, using the try square, that the boards line up. Also, make sure the holes for the bolts are exactly centred, i.e. for 18 mm (¾ in.) wide board, centre at 9 mm (⅜ in.) (fig. 2).
- Mark up the centres for the dowels, taking care not to put them close to the edge of the board.
- Put the sides together in a vice/Workmate /cramp and drill through the hole for the bolt, making sure the drill is held vertically.
- Drill the hole for the dowel.
- Once all the holes are drilled, the sides can be assembled. Line up the dowel using a slotted screwdriver, and insert the bolt with a hex/Allen key (fig. 4).
- The top can be made with a flange (fig. 3), to avoid the need for top fixings.
- Similar to above, mark out as in fig. 5. Remember that the hole for the insert nut will be larger than that for the bolt.
  Cross-dowel bolt and insert nut.
- The nut is inserted using a hex/Allen key.
- Alternatively, a countersunk bolt could be used as in fig. 6.

FLAT-PACKS

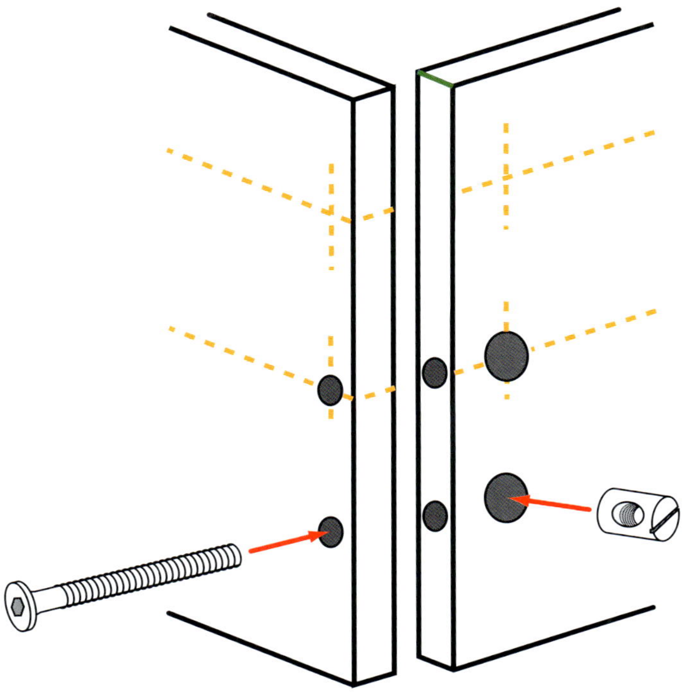

fig. 1

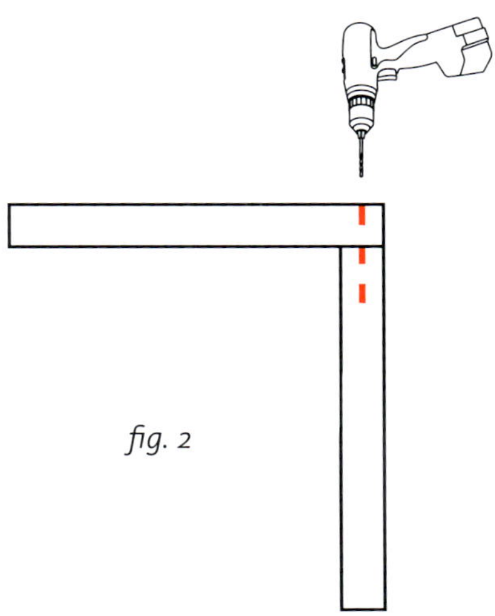

fig. 2

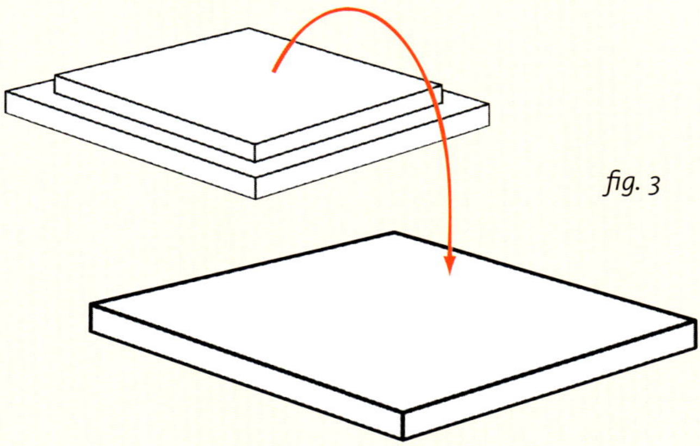

fig. 3

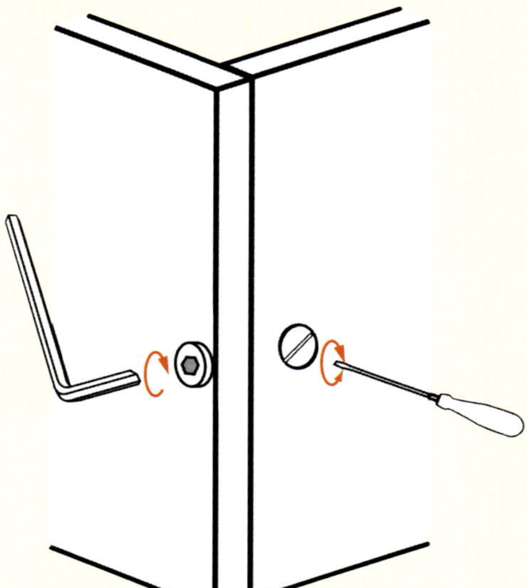

fig. 4

FLAT-PACKS

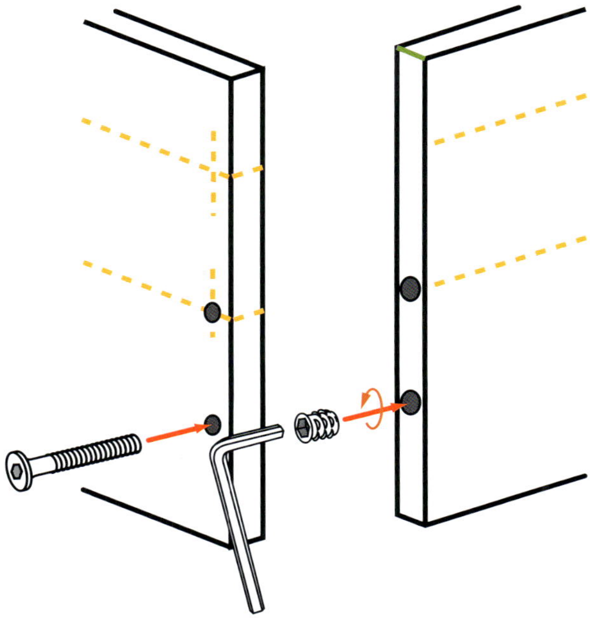

fig. 5

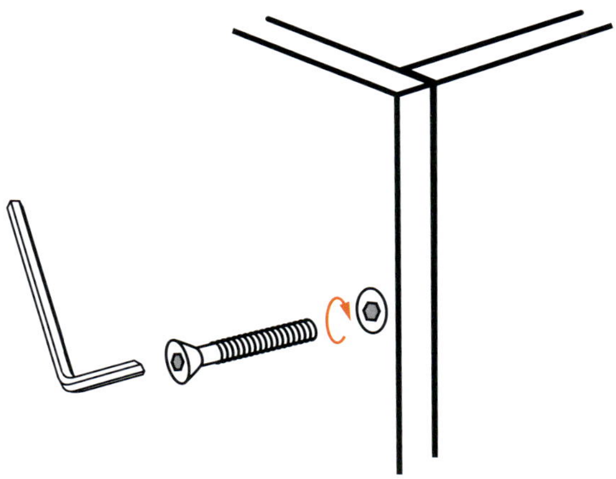

fig. 6

MAKING A SHELF

(See Making a Plinth, page 142).
This first shelf, with triangular sides, is ideal for heavy objects, providing it is securely fixed to the wall.

Depending on the size and load of the shelf, use either 12 or 18 mm (½ or ¾ in.) MDF (or other sheet wood as desired).

Decide on the size and make the cutting list. The height of the back should be 12 or 18 mm (½ or ¾ in.) less than the top (depending on the thickness of the board). This height will also define the size of the two triangles used for the sides (see fig. 1).

- Place the back in a vice and run some glue along the top edge (fig. 2).

- Take the top and position one edge along one edge of the back. Drill and countersink at least two holes, 6 or 9 mm (¼ or ¾ in.) in from the edge and 60 mm (2½ in.) along from the corners (figs 3 & 4).

- Screw in the screws using size 4 x 35–40 mm (size 8 x 1⅜–1⅝ in.) countersunk screws (fig. 5).

- Attach the two sides, ensuring that the screws are not too near the points of the triangles (fig. 6).

- Finish/paint as required.

HANGING A SHELF

Now you've got your shelf, the next step is to hang it on the wall.

MAKING A SHELF

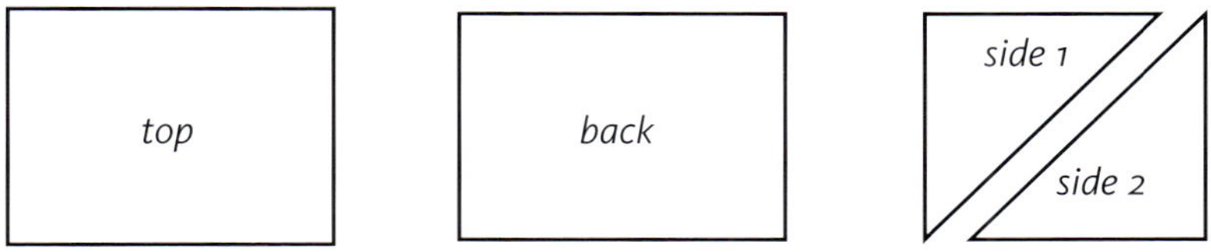

fig. 1

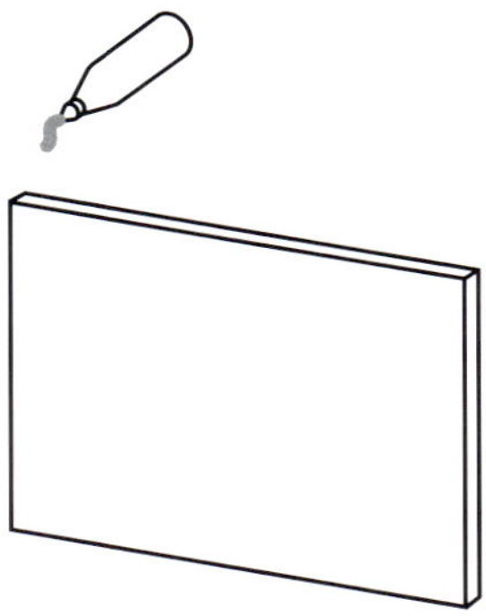

fig. 2

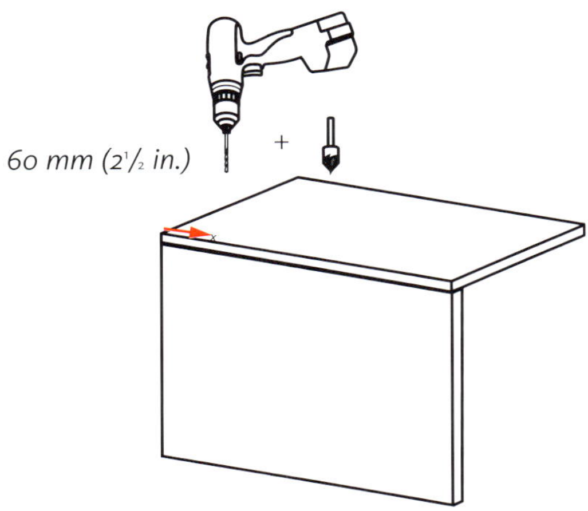

fig. 3

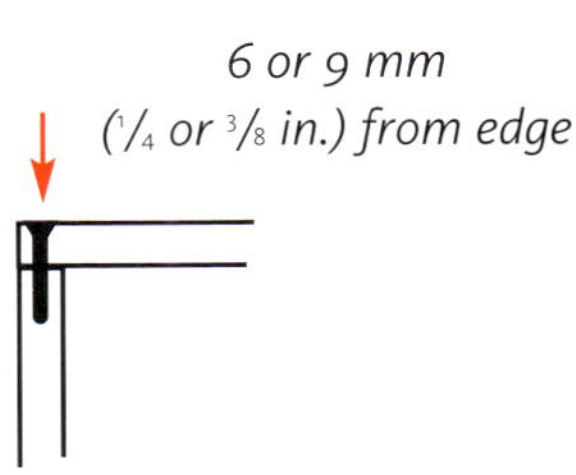

fig. 4

Decide on the type of fixing you will require (see relevant pages). You may be able to use one really secure fixing, with the others just adding stability. For example, one Rawlbolt will carry such a heavy load that you may only need a couple of other Rawlplug fixings to stop the shelf from swivelling (see fig. 1).

- Drill the appropriate-size holes in the back of the shelf (fig. 2).
- Offer up the shelf to the wall, then level using a spirit level, and mark the position with a pencil (though I quite often use a drill bit).
- Drill the necessary holes in the wall (fig. 4).
- Screw in fixings as required, checking that the shelf is still level (fig. 5).

NB It's sometimes easier to position one hole, drill and fix, then re-level and mark out the other holes, take down, drill holes in the wall and re-fix.

These instructions can be applied to most shelves, whether you have made them or not, including those that use shelf brackets.

MAKING A SHELF

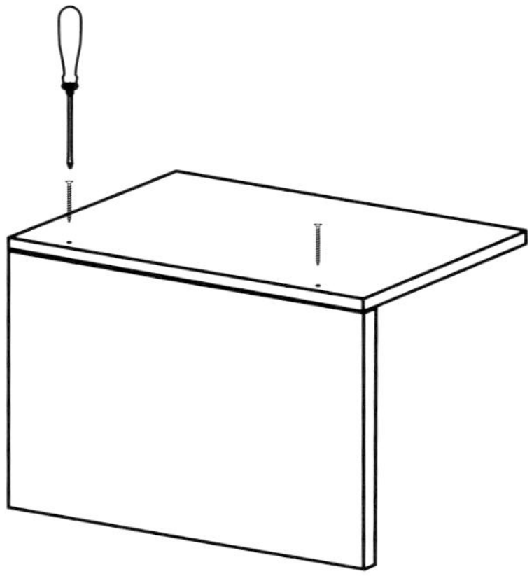

fig. 5

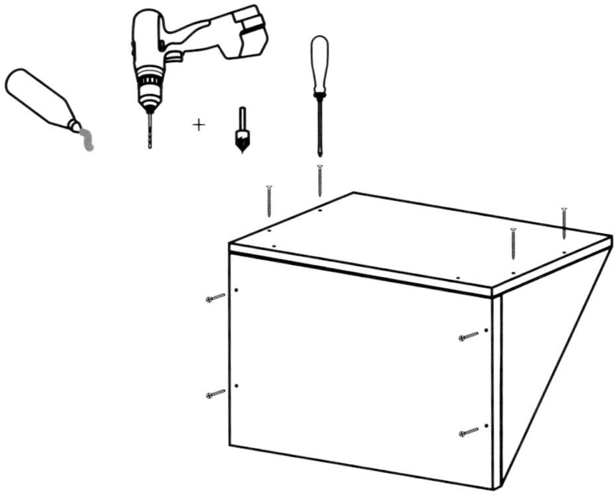

fig. 6

HANGING A SHELF

? fixing type, e.g.

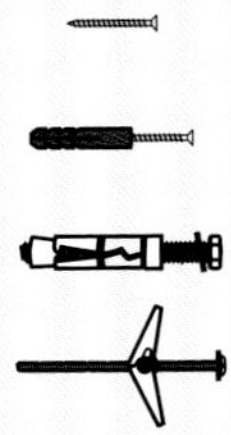

fig. 1

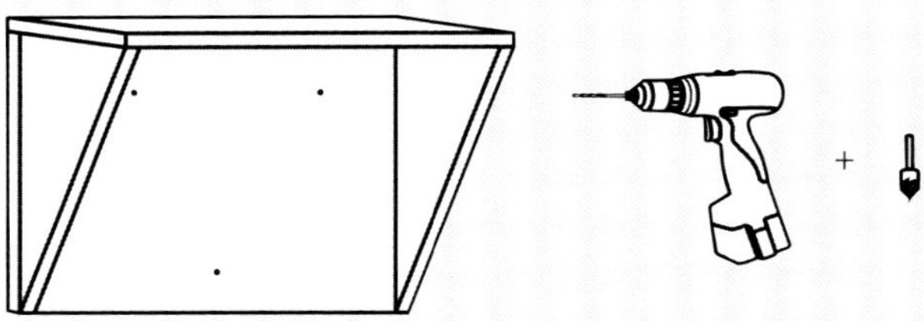

(if needed)

fig. 2

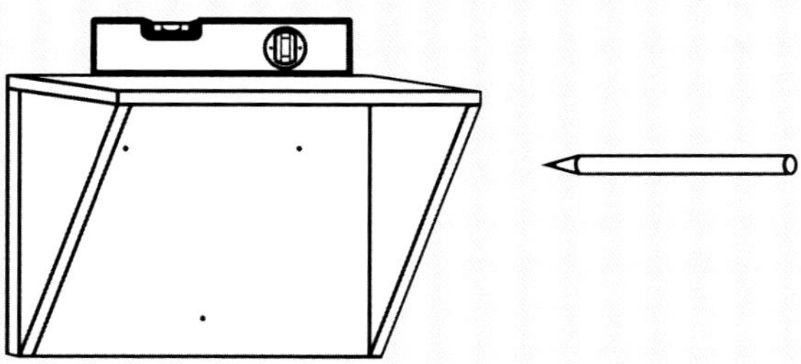

fig. 2

HANGING A SHELF

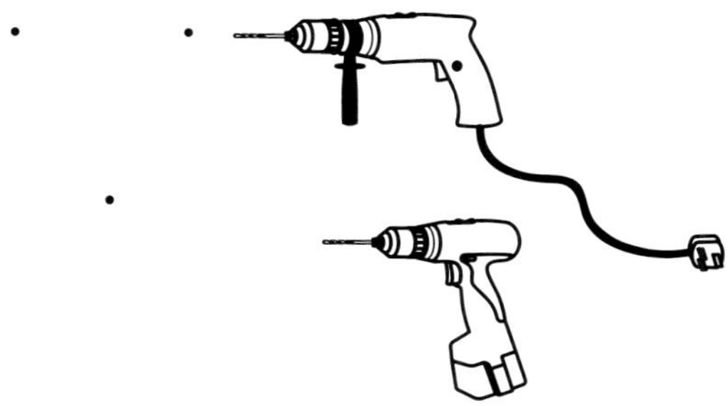

fig. 4

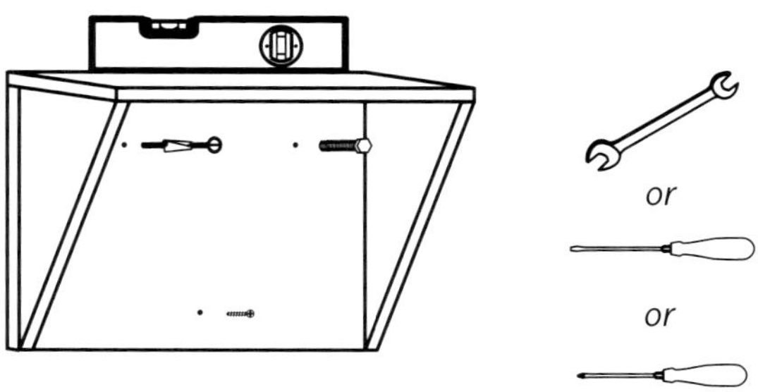

fig. 5

MAKING AND HANGING A BOX SHELF

(See Making a Plinth and Making a Shelf, pages 142 & 158)

This shelf is designed for lighter loads, so 12 mm (½ in.) MDF (or other sheet wood as desired) will be more than adequate. The base is optional, depending on your aesthetics.

Decide on the size and make a cutting list. The front and back panels should be the same length as the top, with the sides 24 mm (1 in.) less than the width of the top (see fig. 1). I would suggest that the depth of the shelf be between 75 and 100 mm (3 and 4 in.). The greater the depth, the more load the shelf will be able to carry.

- Place the back in a vice and run some glue along the top edge. Take the top and position the glued edge along one of the back edges. Drill and countersink at least two holes 6 mm (¼ in.) in from the edge and 60 mm (2½ in.) along from the corners. Screw in the screws using size 4 x 35–40 mm (size 8 x 1⅜–1⅝ in.) countersunk screws (fig. 2). Do the same with the front.

- Attach the two sides, gluing and screwing in from the top (fig. 3). However, you only need to glue the corner joints between the sides and front and back, holding them together with masking tape until the glue dries (fig. 4). It's best not to screw this joint, as you run the risk of splitting the wood.

- Turn over the shelf and put the base (optional) in place. Drill the holes for fixing, but do not glue or put the screws in at this point (fig. 5).

BOX SHELF – MAKING

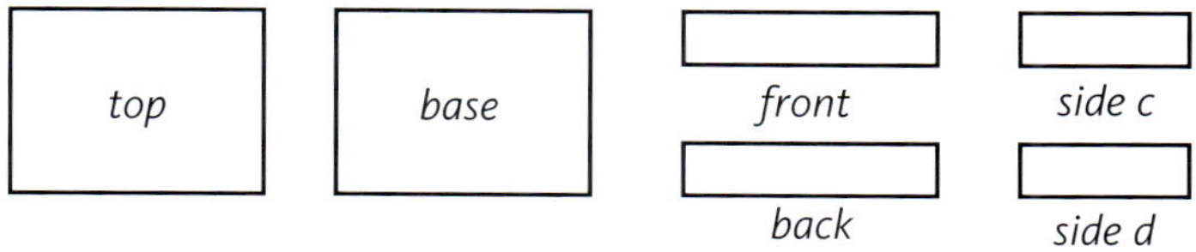

fig. 1

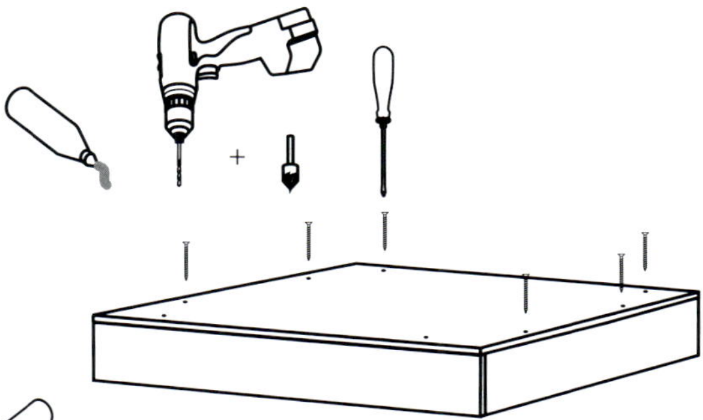

fig. 3

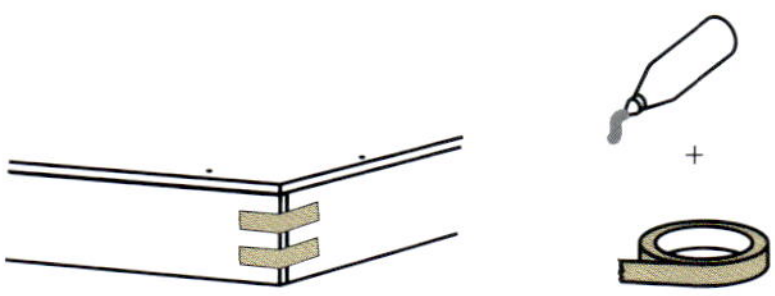

fig. 4

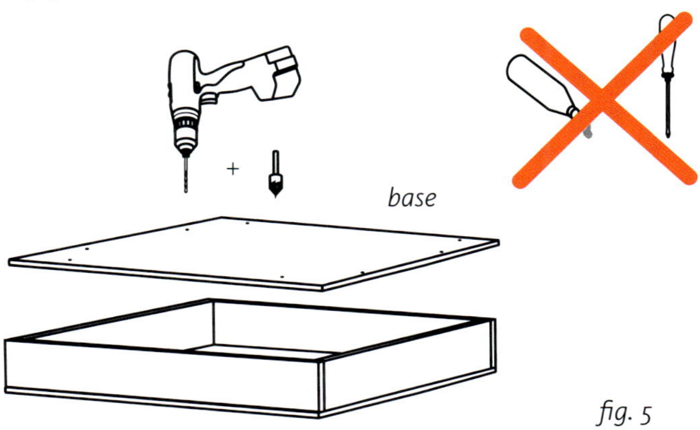

fig. 5

- Choose the relevant fixings, mark and level, then fix the shelf to the wall (fig. 6).

Finally, if you have chosen to add a base, screw it into place – but don't glue, as you will have to remove it in order to take down the shelf at the end of the show (fig. 7).

NB Gluing and taping is a perfectly good way of putting together small structures and is particularly good if you are using board that is thinner than 12 mm (½ in.), which is likely to split if screwed or pinned.

see Hanging a shelf

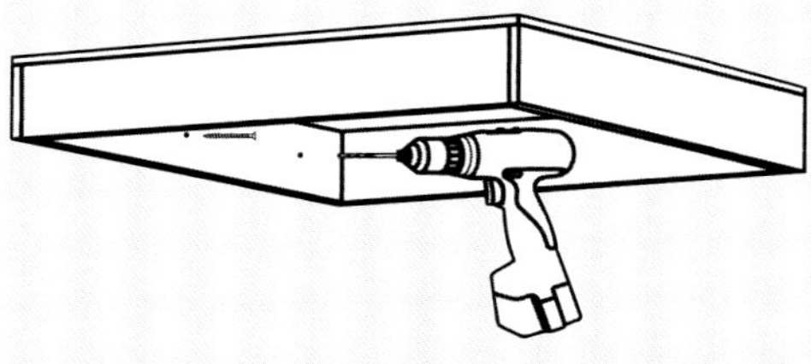

fig. 6

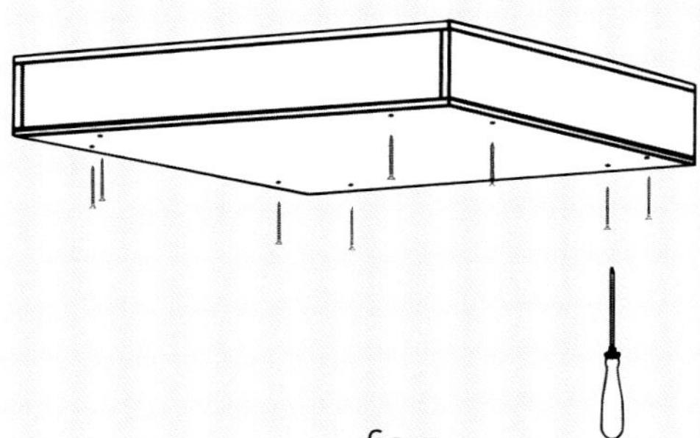

fig. 7

9

stage nine

electrics – uk, european, n. american
cable management
lighting

notes

ELECTRICS

SAFETY

The electricity supply in the UK is 240 V, so if you get an electric shock from an appliance, plug or lead, it is potentially fatal. Electrical systems are designed with this in mind, but obviously care needs to be taken when carrying out any installation that involves the use of electricity.

All items that have a plug on them, including extension leads, should preferably be PAT (Portable Appliance Testing) tested by a competent electrician or someone trained in PAT testing. You should carry out a visual check on all items to include:

- Checking the casing of the equipment – is it in good condition or is it cracked or broken?
- Checking the cable – look for cuts or signs of the cable being squashed.
- Checking that it is fitted with a UK 240 V, 13 amp, 3-pin plug with both the live and neutral pins insulated?
- Checking that it has the appropriate fuse fitted for the item you are using, i.e. 3, 5 or 13 amp (see chart below).

Fuse rating	Colour	Load (watts)
3 amp	red	< 700
5 amp	grey	>700 < 1200
13 amp	brown	>1200 < 3000

notes

- Check that the plug is wired correctly (unless it is a moulded plug):

Brown = live cable to live pin
Blue = neutral cable to neutral pin
Green/yellow = earth cable to earth pin

- The inner sleeves should go all the way to the terminals with no bare wire showing or any nicks or cuts.
- The outer sleeve/casing should be secured in the plug with the cable grip.
- If the equipment fails any of these requirements it should not be used.

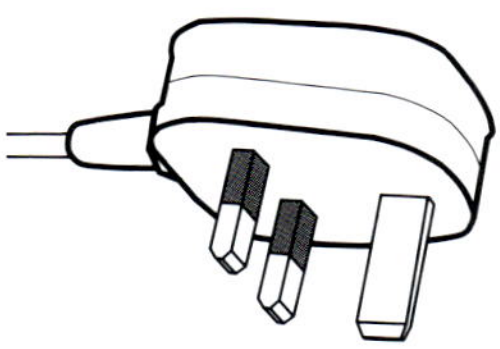

UK 3-pin plug

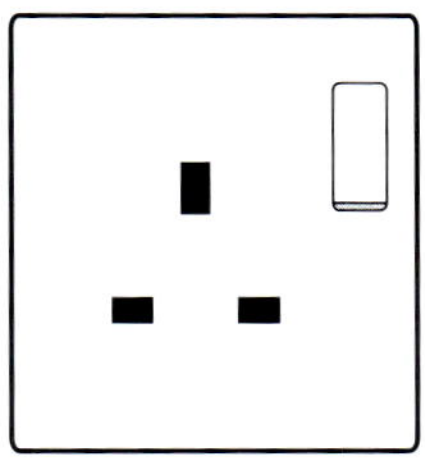

UK switched socket

- Note: Many items are fitted with moulded plugs that cannot be opened. You should, however, still check the fuse, which is certainly accessible. Some items, such as power tools, are double-insulated and have no earth lead. A double-insulated item will be marked with the symbol of a square within a square.

- To decrease the risk of accidental shock, it is sometimes wise to use an RCD unit (residual current device), which plugs into the socket. If there is any fault in the wiring then the RCD will automatically cut the power before you get electrocuted. It's a good idea to use one with power tools, when there is a risk of cutting through cable, and a must when running exterior cable, or cable in damp conditions, or when water is involved in an installation. Many galleries will insist on the use of an RCD.

NB Safety with electrics should be taken very seriously – galleries and other venues will insist upon it. See also Risk Assessment (page 10).

WIRING PLUGS

- Take off the back of the plug by unscrewing the larger screw in the centre.
- Prepare the cable, taking care not to cut into the inner cables when cutting back the outer sheathing.
- Use a sharp knife and cut down the length of the sheathing to the required length, between 4 and 5 cm (about 2 in.) should suffice (fig. 1).
- Peel back the sheathing and cut it off.
- Alternatively, you can score around the sheathing at the desired point, then, flexing the cable, pull the sheathing at the same time so that it breaks through.

WIRING A PLUG

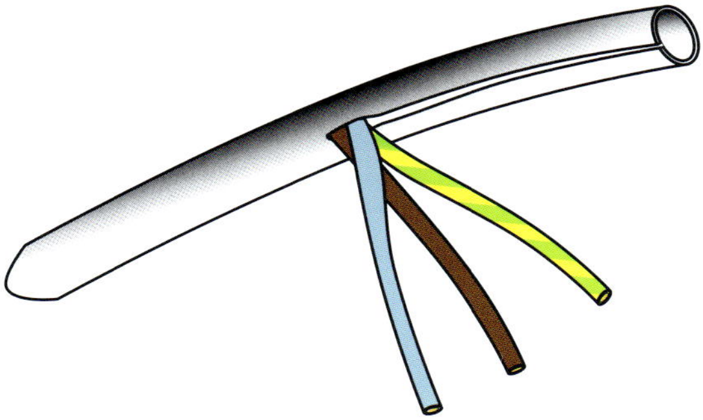

fig. 1

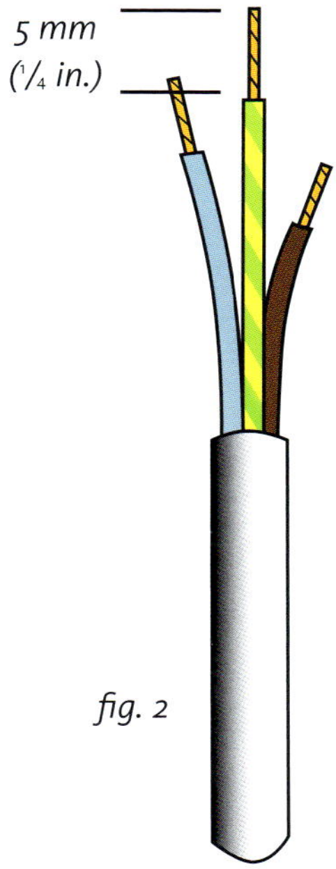

fig. 2

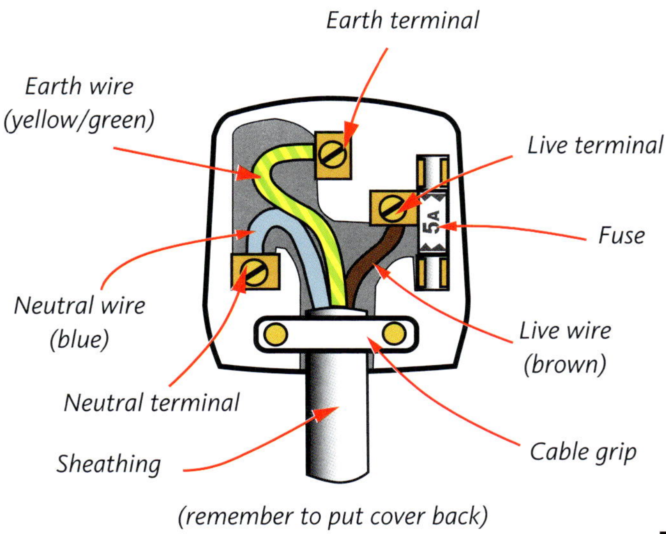

fig. 3

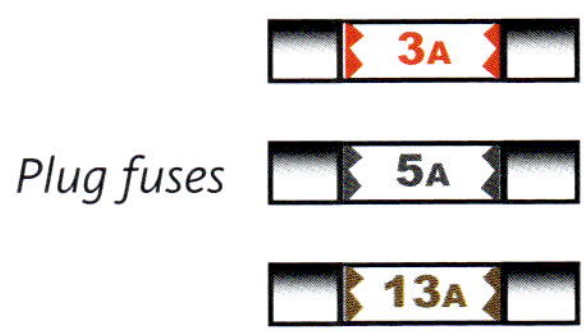

fig. 4

- The inner cables should then be cut to the right lengths (the live wire is usually shorter than the neutral and the earth).

- Remove about 5 mm (¼ in.) of insulation from the end of each cable using wire strippers/cutters, being careful not to cut into the individual strands of wire. Twist the exposed wire so as not to have any loose strands (fig. 2).

- The inner cables are then attached to the correct terminals:

Brown >	Live
Blue >	Neutral
Green/yellow >	Earth

- Slacken the screw, push the bare cable into the hole and tighten the screw (fig. 3).

- Make sure there are no bare wires or loose strands of wire showing.

TIP: It is easier to get the cable into the hole if you push the pins up slightly. Some plugs have clamps, so wrap the wire clockwise around the post and tighten the clamp.

- Make sure the sheathing is held firmly in place with the cord grip.

- Again, always check that you have the appropriate fuse for the appliance (see chart above, and also fig. 4).

- Some loads may need a slightly higher-rated fuse than normal, e.g. a 500 W halogen light should be fitted with a 5 amp fuse.
- Before screwing on the back cover, make sure that the wires are lying in the correct channels and will not be pinched when the cover is replaced.
- Double-check all is correct and replace the back cover, tightening up the screw.

EXTENSION LEADS

- Check the length of the cable for cuts. The cable should be the correct size to carry the current of the equipment they are being used for, so look on the equipment for its power usage (load), which is measured in watts (W). If you're running more than one item from an extension, add up the total wattage.
- Extension leads should have a switch on the socket end.
- They should also be the appropriate length. Do not stretch cable, or have so much excess that it needs coiling. If you are using an extension drum, it should be fully unwound (to prevent possible overheating).
- Adaptor blocks should not be used.
- Always use flex, i.e. flexible cable.
- Do not use solid-core cable, which is flatter and stiffer. This is made for permanent wiring and is not designed for repeated flexing and movement. Flex is made from braided cable.

Choosing flex Flex is rated according to the size of the internal cables

Size	Load
0.5 mm	720 W
0.75 mm	1440 W
1.0 mm	2400 W
1.25 mm	3120 W
1.5 mm	3600 W
2.5 mm	4800 W

- It's worth noting that manufacturers usually fit appliances with a load of less than 3000 W (3 kW) with 1.25 mm flex. It is safer and more sensible to choose a larger flex over a smaller one, especially with extension leads.

- If you are making up an extension lead, use 1.5 mm cable with a 13 amp fuse. This will allow for a wide range of equipment, without the risk of overloading.

- Wire up the trailing socket (2 or 4 gang, etc.), checking that the live, neutral and earth wires go to the correct pins/terminals, and that you use the cable grip (see Wiring plugs).

- Make sure that the cable is in one piece, i.e. from plug to socket. However, if you do need to join cable, use a proper in-line flex connector (fig. 1).

- You can join up extension leads, plug to socket, although this is rather cumbersome and does not look great.

- Never use the simple plastic block connectors (chocolate blocks) (see fig. 2).

CABLE CONNECTIONS

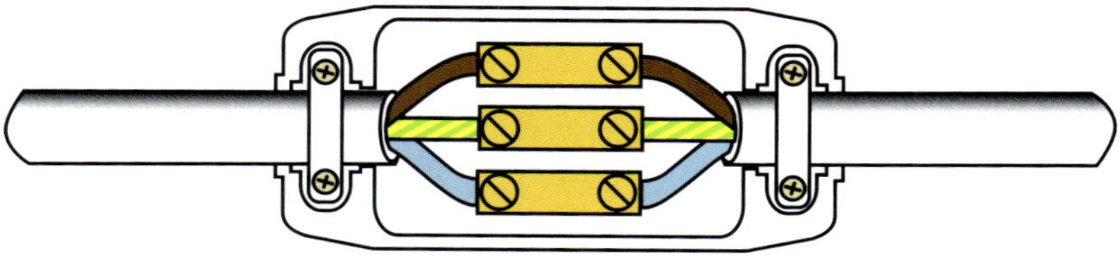

In-line connector (remember to put the cover back)

fig. 1

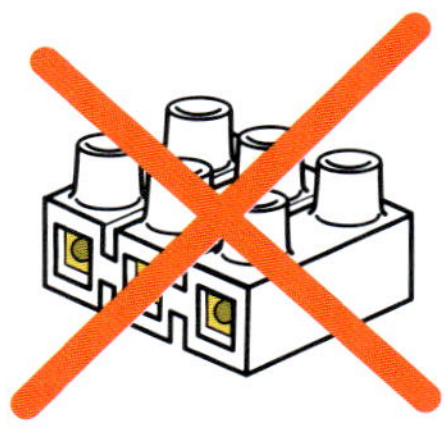

Plastic block (chocolate block)

fig. 2

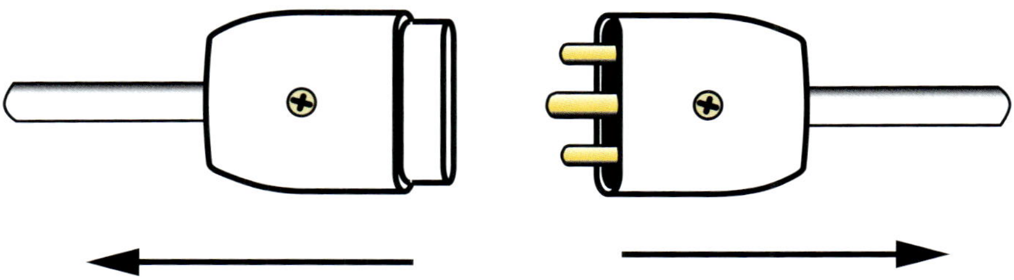

Two-part flex connector

fig. 3

- If you're using two-part flex connectors, make sure that the side with the pins is on the socket side, never the plug side (fig. 3). These are normally used, where necessary, in AV installations.

CABLE MANAGEMENT

LAYING CABLE

Think about where the cable is going to and from, keeping it simple and tidy; cable should always run vertically up or down walls, never diagonally. All the cable should be secure, not dangling from walls or presenting a possible trip hazard on the floor. There are various means of doing this (see below).

If you are laying cable to an object in the middle of the floor, there should be as little cable run on the floor as possible – take it back to the wall at the nearest point. Also, it must always be covered.

- Plastic conduit/mini-trunking is available in several sizes. You can buy it in lengths or in rolls, and it's easy to cut to size. There are self-sticking types. If you don't like the look of cable, conduit offers a neat solution, and is good for running up or along the bottom of walls. However, it should not be used on the floor (fig. 1).

- Plastic cable clips (with nails), are available in various sizes; make sure to buy the correct size for the cable you are running. Nail a clip about every 400 mm (16 in.) (fig. 2).

- Self-adhesive cable clip. Cable clips can sometimes be difficult to nail, particularly on masonry or brick walls. In this instance,

CABLE MANAGEMENT

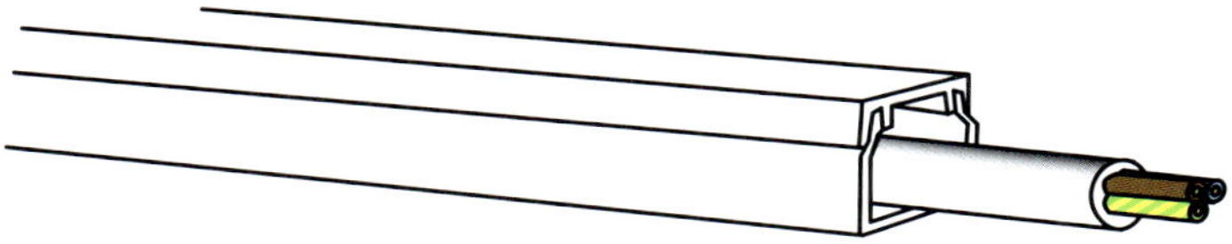

Mini-trunking

fig. 1

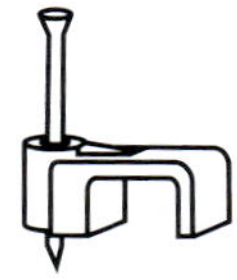

Plastic cable clip

fig. 2

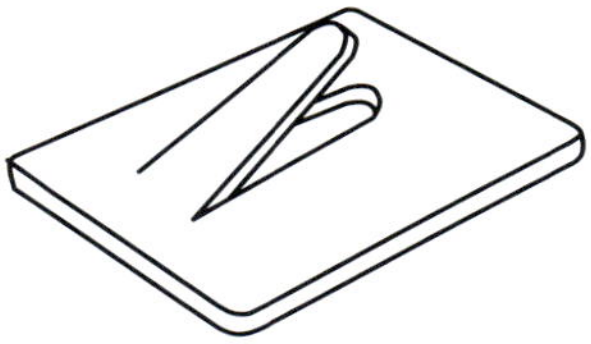

Self-adhesive cable clip

fig. 3

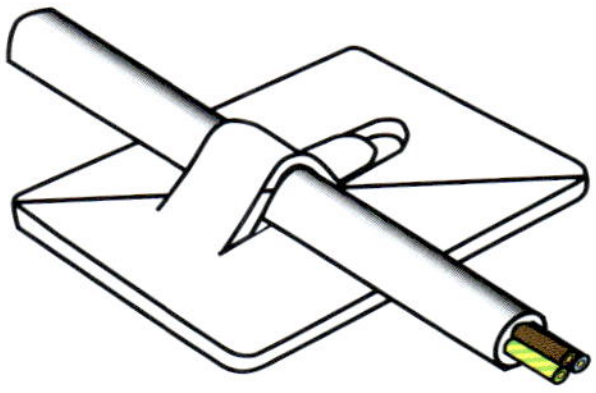

fig. 4

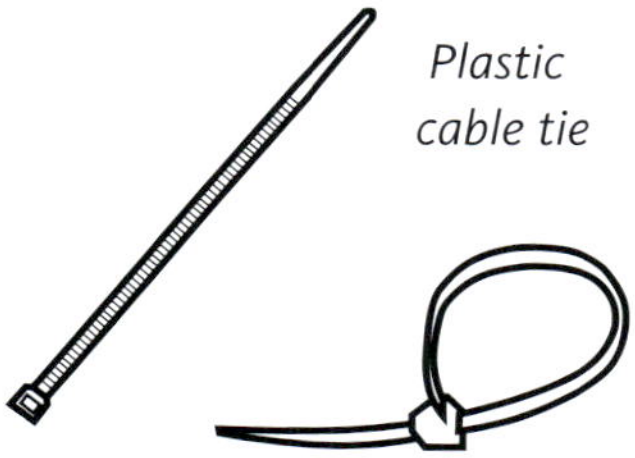

fig. 5

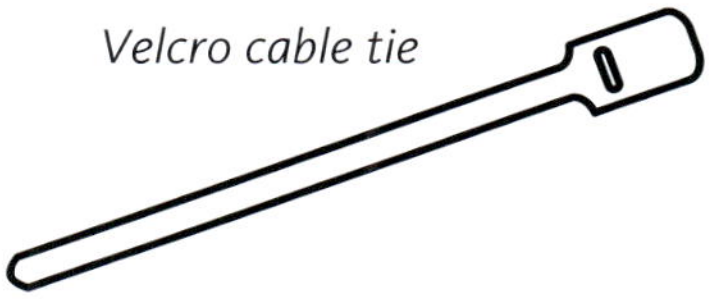

fig. 6

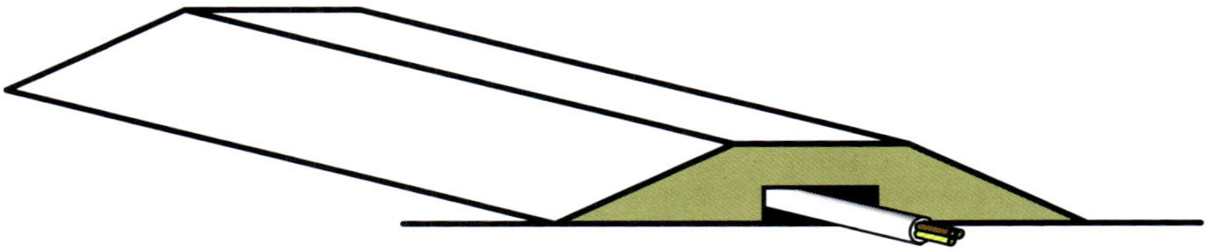

Cable cover (floor)

fig. 7

you can use sticky-pad clips, which are also good if you want to avoid hammering walls where there may be a danger of dislodging already installed work. These are very easy and quick to use and are particularly good for temporary installations (figs 3 & 4).

- Cable ties can be used to attach cable to existing items. It's always worth keeping a few ties in your toolbox – they are handy for all sorts of things. Also available are self-adhesive bases made to thread ties through (fig. 5).

- Velcro cable ties are also available now. These are useful items with the advantage that they can be reused over and over. They can also be stapled onto board walls (fig. 6).

- Wrap-back ties are double-sided Velcro (hook and loop fastener), which is sold in rolls or by the metre. Ties are a great way of keeping several cables tidy, for example in AV set-ups.

- Gaffer tape. Use it with care, as it can look very messy, particularly on walls. It is advisable, however, to gaffer-tape any cable to the floor before you cover it.

TIP: It is a good idea to cover the cable with masking tape before the gaffer, as gaffer tape leaves a sticky residue when removed from the cable.

- Cable floor cover. If the exhibition is open to the public, or the cable is likely to be trodden on, then it should be covered with a rubber cable cover. This is quite expensive, so one alternative is to make a cover from strips of board with angled edges and a groove to hide the cable. Both have the advantage that they can be painted the same colour as the floor (fig. 7).

LIGHTING

Lighting is a tricky subject. If you're showing within a gallery, then the gallery manager or the technician should always be consulted before you start making any adjustments to the lighting. If you're showing in a space that is not a formal gallery setting, I would always advise against adding any lighting unless it's absolutely necessary, go with what you've got.

People often install temporary domestic lights, spots and the like, which generally do little for the work and look out of place. Good-quality lighting is expensive, and installing it is a skill in itself. If you do need to install lighting, keep it simple and think about how it will look with the work. Consider sight lines, as you don't want to dazzle the viewer!

Do not attempt to wire into existing lighting circuits; always run temporary lighting from power sockets.

Current law means that any interference with circuits can only be done by a qualified electrician, who will have to issue a certificate.

Lighting can be run in sequence, i.e. each light can be run on from the one next to it. Using 1.0 or 1.5 mm cable and a 5 amp fuse, you could run up to 12 x 100 W bulbs. It's sometimes possible to link lights together directly, but it's often easier to use junction boxes (see the lighting circuits diagram). This method can also be used for wiring a sequence of light boxes.

Remember that light bulbs give off heat; the higher the wattage, the hotter the bulb. Never place bulbs near flammable materials or where there is a risk of people being burnt.

Halogen floodlights are often used, being cheap and offering a high level of light output. They are, however, extremely hot and will burn skin upon contact. So bearing in mind that children visit public exhibitions, you should never use this kind of lighting on the floor or low down on walls. Always make sure that the cable is kept away from the body of the light. Also, given that they have a high load, it is advisable to run them singly, not in sequence. Because they are so bright, care should be taken when deciding where to site them.

Fluorescent lights are much cooler and can be fitted with daylight tubes. Although not to everyone's taste, they do give a good spread of light and are easier to site.

If you're using pendant lights, try using the energy-efficient type of bulb; not are they only more environmentally friendly than the older type, they are also a lot cooler.

When wiring up lights, remember that the same rules apply as before: check that live is going to live, etc., and do not leave any exposed cable, using cord grips if there are some (though as most lights are sold to be used as fixed items and are usually fed from above, very few will have a cord grip). Fluorescent and halogen floods usually have simple plastic blocks to wire up to (see the light connections diagram, fig. 1).

If the fittings are made to be fed from above, it

LIGHTING CIRCUITS

Temporary lighting circuit
Lights wired in sequences with junction boxes

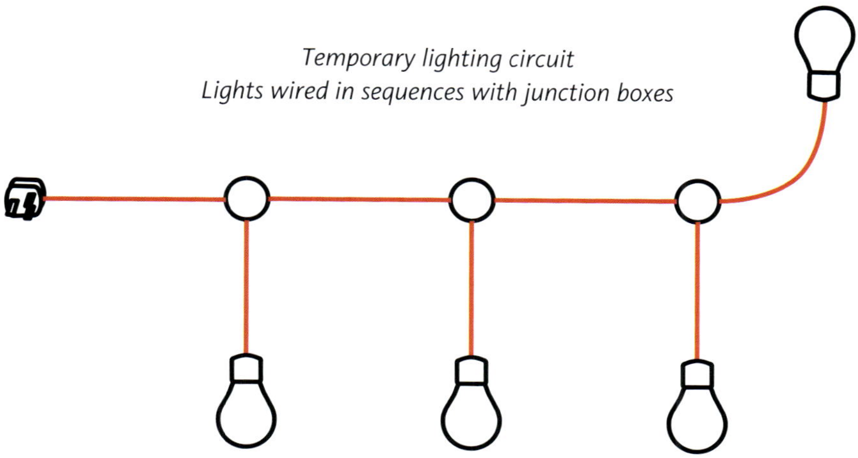

Junction-box wiring

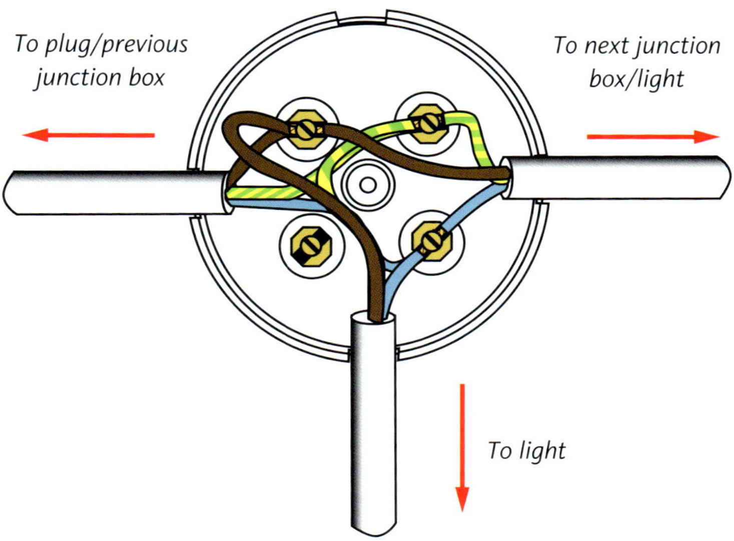

NB Always put the covers back on the junction boxes

may be necessary to fix the light fitting onto a block, so that the cable can be fed into it. Do not squash the cable between the ceiling and the casing. Make sure when wiring pendant lights (fig. 2) that the inner cables wrap under the shoulders, otherwise the weight of the fitting will pull on the terminals. Also, remember to put the top cover on the flex before wiring.

MODIFYING ELECTRICAL APPLIANCES

If you want to modify a 240 V appliance to serve another purpose, seek advice before you begin. The appliance is unlikely to pass any risk-assessment process unless it has first been PAT-certified. I have known people waste enormous amounts of time making work which then proved unsafe to exhibit.

It is standard practice for motor-driven work to run with a 12 V supply, using a transformer. 12 V motors are readily available – cars run off the same voltage, so things like windscreen-wiper motors can be adapted to suit.

If you are using 240 V motors, their application should be discussed, advice should be sought, and they must be PAT-tested.

EUROPEAN ELECTRICS (NON UK)

The electricity supply in European countries is between 220 – 240 V so, as in the UK, electric shock can be fatal.

The main difference between UK and European electrics is the types of plugs and sockets used. Apart from this, both comply with standard

LIGHT CONNECTIONS

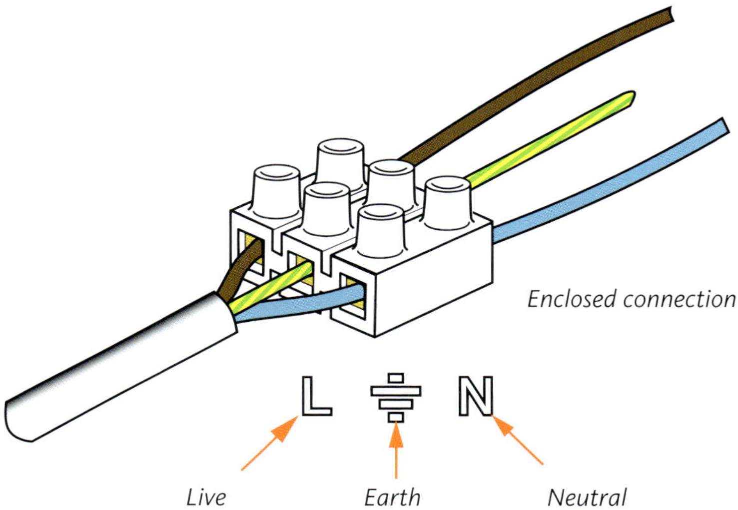

fig. 1

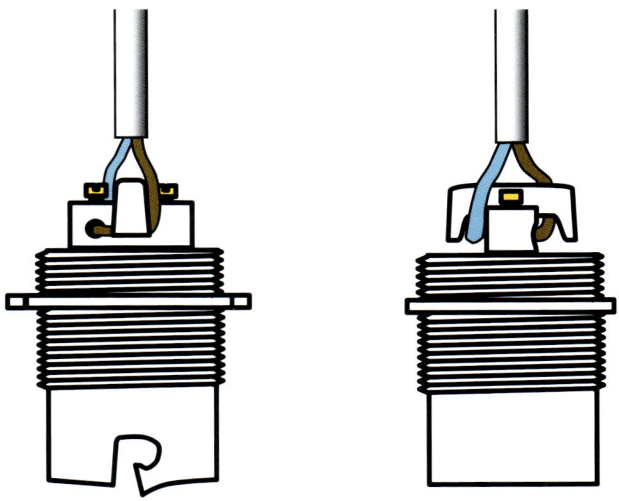

Pendant light connection
NB Fitting shown without top or bottom cover

fig. 2

European use of flex, cable, etc. (Refer to main Electrics section). There are a variety of plugs in use in European countries and the three most common are: Type C, Type E, Type F (hybrid), all shown opposite. You may find some variations from these in certain countries. Unlike UK plugs, they do not have internal fuses and because European sockets are unswitched they are non-polarized, meaning that the live and neutral wires can be interchanged. In practice it is common to wire plugs with live on the left and neutral on the right, but check for variations.

Type C plugs, commonly known as 'europlugs' have two pins and are used in class 2 products (do not require earthing and are double insulated) and require up to 2.5 A. They will fit into Type C, Type E and Type F sockets.

Type E plugs have two pins and a female earth, the socket having a male earth pin.

Type F 'schucko' plugs have two pins and have earth clips top and bottom. These days most moulded plugs (factory fitted) and good quality replacement plugs of this type are a hybrid version, having the addition of a female earth hole which allows them to be used in French type sockets. Type E, F and hybrid E/F plugs are rated at 16 amps.

WIRING PLUGS

- Undo the body of the plug to access the terminals.

- Prepare the cable, taking care not to cut into the inner cables when cutting back the outer sheathing.

EUROPEAN PLUGS AND SOCKETS

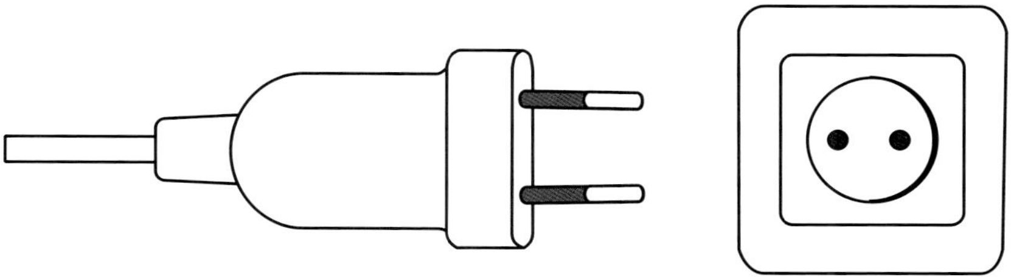

Type C (European 2-pin) plug socket

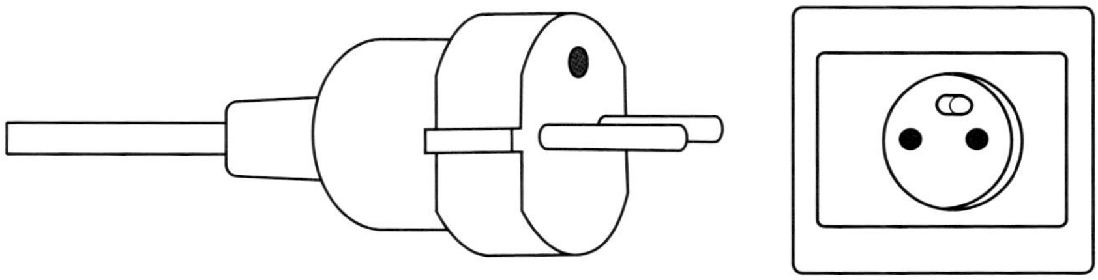

Type E (French 2-pin, female earth) plug and socket

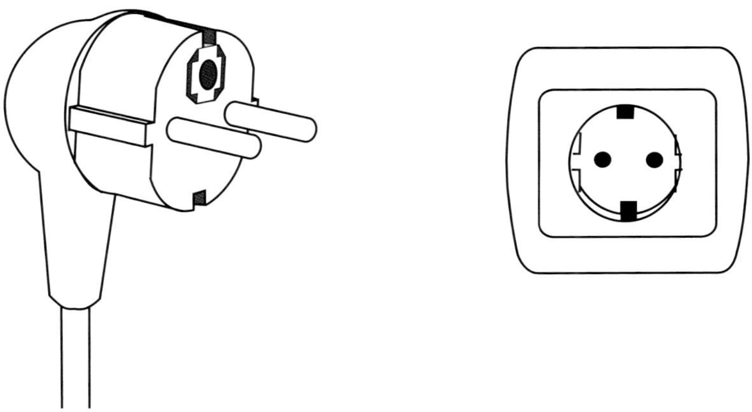

Type E/F hybrid (2-pin, side clip earth + female earth) plug and Type F socket

- Use a sharp knife and cut down the length of the sheathing to the required length, 4–5 cm (2 in.) should suffice (fig. 1).
- Peel back the sheathing and cut off.
- Alternatively, you can score around the sheathing at the desired point, then flex the cable pulling the sheathing at the same time so that it breaks through.
- The inner cables should then be cut to the right lengths.
- Remove about 5 mm (¼ in.) of insulation from the end of each cable using wire strippers/cutters, being careful not to cut into the individual strands of wire. Twist the exposed wire, so not to have any loose strands (fig. 2).
- The inner cables are then attached to the correct terminals (fig. 3). It is usual to attach the live wire to the left side as shown. Slacken the screw, push the bare cable into the hole and tighten the screw.
- Make sure there are no bare wires or loose strands of wire showing.
- Replace the cover, making sure that the sheathing is within the plug and is held in place with the cord grip.

AMERICAN ELECTRICS

Unlike in the UK and Europe, North American (and Japanese) electricity supply is 110–120 V, which is a safer voltage, although care should still be taken to avoid electric shock. It should be noted that some large equipment such as water

WIRING A PLUG, EUROPEAN

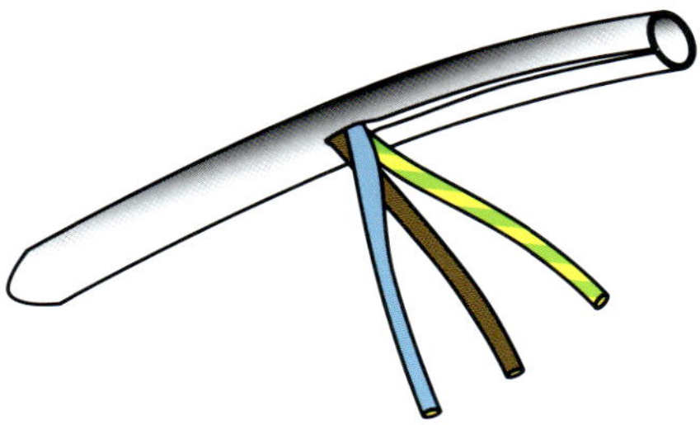

fig. 1

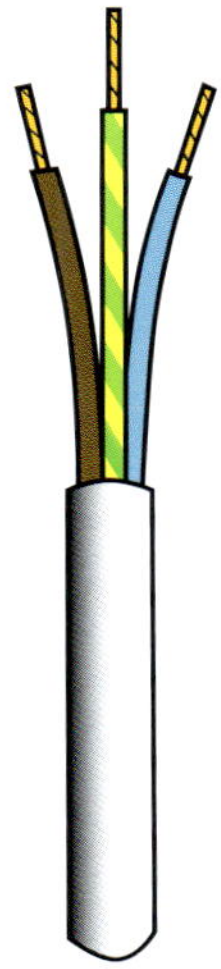

fig. 2

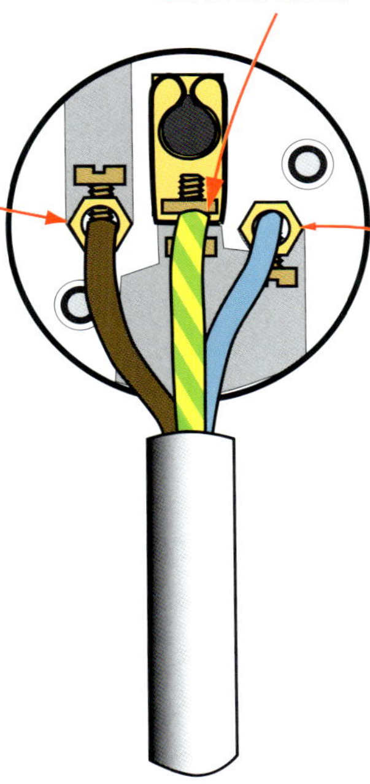

fig. 3

heaters are rated at 240 V (this is achieved by combining two 120 V lines at the service panel).

- Always check equipment and leads/cords for damage before use.

- Many items are fitted with moulded plugs that cannot be opened. Some equipment, such as power tools are double insulated and have no earth lead.

- Check that plugs are wired properly (unless using a moulded plug).

Black›	Live/Hot
White›	Neutral/Cold
Green›	Earth/Ground

- American plugs are not fused.

(see also safety section at the beginning of this stage).

The two most used types of plugs in America are the Type A two-pin and Type B three-pin/U-ground.

Type A plugs are used for lamps and small double insulated appliances, such as power tools. Most now have the neutral blade wider than the live, meaning they can only be inserted one way into either type A or B sockets/outlets.

Type B plugs have two parallel blades, the neutral blade wider than the live, with a round earth/ground blade.

Both are rated at 15 amps.

AMERICAN PLUGS AND SOCKETS/RECEPTACLES

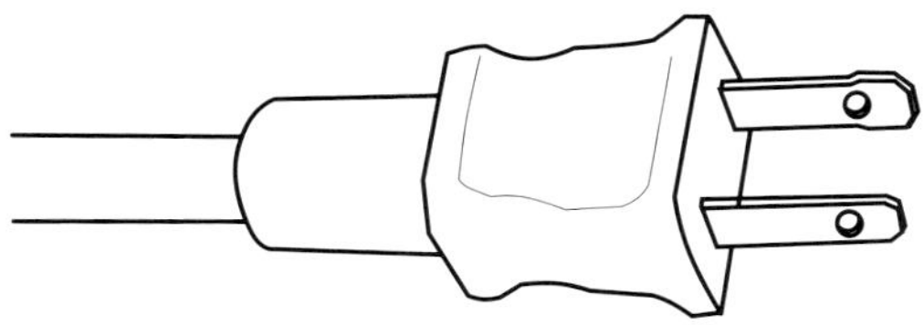

Type A 2-pin/blade plug

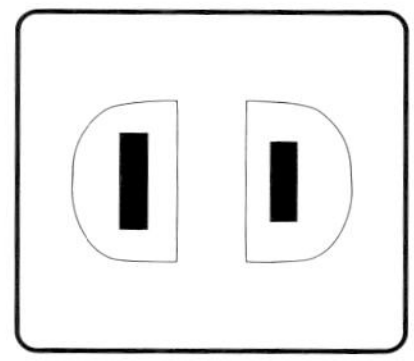

Type A receptacle

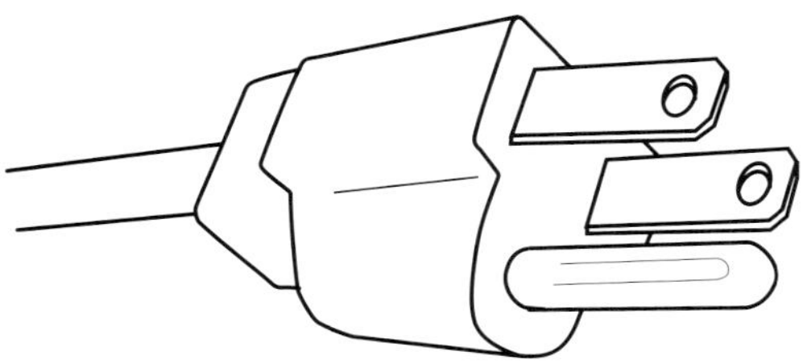

Type B 2-pin/blade and ground pin plug

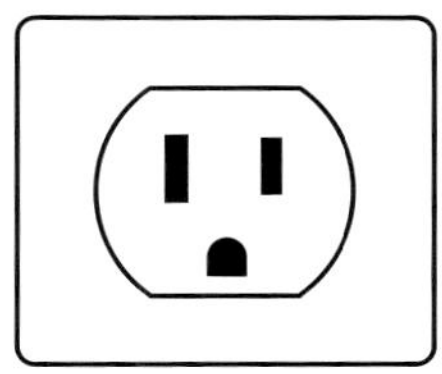

Type B receptacle

WIRING PLUGS (TYPE B)

- Remove the faceplate from the plug and feed the cord through the back of the plug.
- Strip about 75 mm (3 in.) of outer sheathing, revealing the three internal wires, being careful not to cut into these (fig. 1).
- Strip 18 mm (¾ in.) of insulation from the inner wires, then twist the strands together (fig. 2).
- If possible, tie an underwriter's knot (fig. 3) with the black and white (shown blue in diagram) wires, making sure that the knot is as near as possible to the stripped outer sheathing. Then pull the cord back into the body of the plug (fig. 4).
- Partially unscrew the live/hot terminal screw and hook with the stripped end of the black wire clockwise around the shank, then tighten up the screw (fig. 5).
- Follow this procedure for the neutral/cold and earth/ground wires.
- Make sure that there are no loose strands of wire and none of the wires are touching each other.
- Replace the faceplate and secure the cord with the cord grip, checking that none of the inner wires are visible.

EXTENSION CORDS

- Check the length of the cable for cuts. The cable should be the correct size to carry the current of the equipment they are being

WIRING A PLUG, AMERICAN

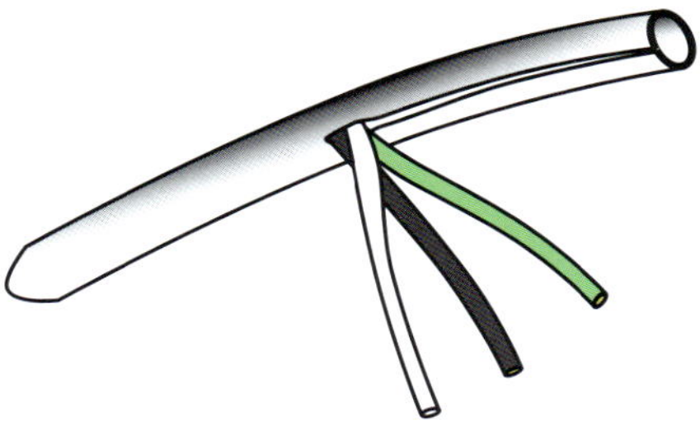

fig. 1

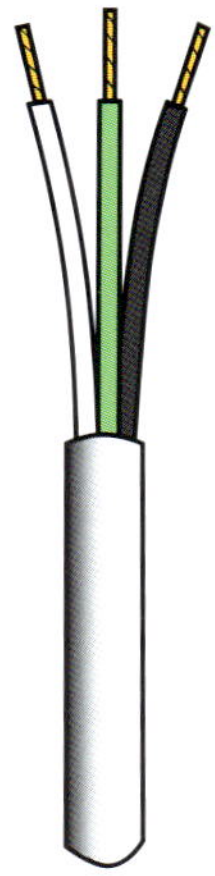

fig. 2

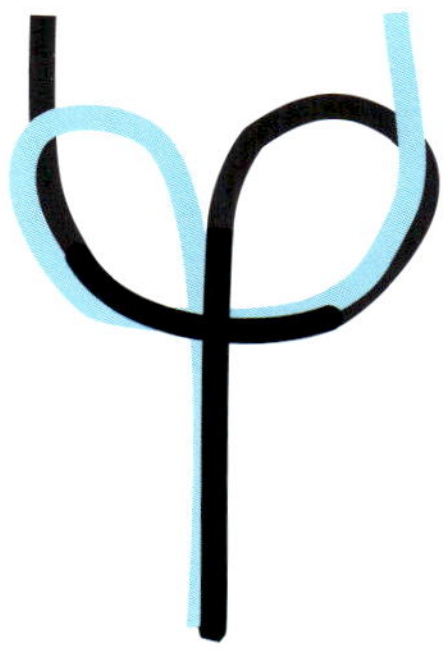

fig. 3

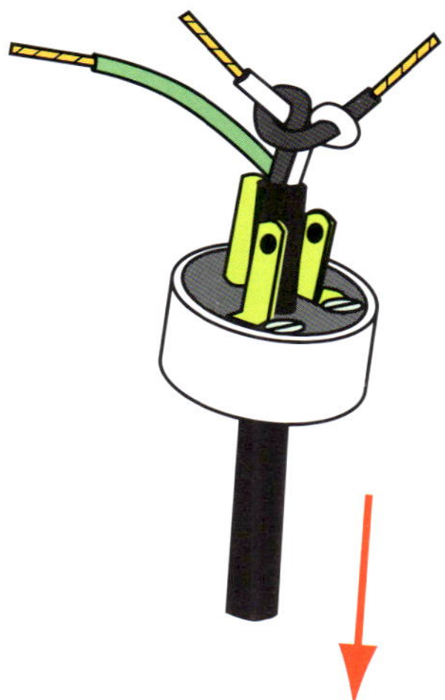

fig. 4

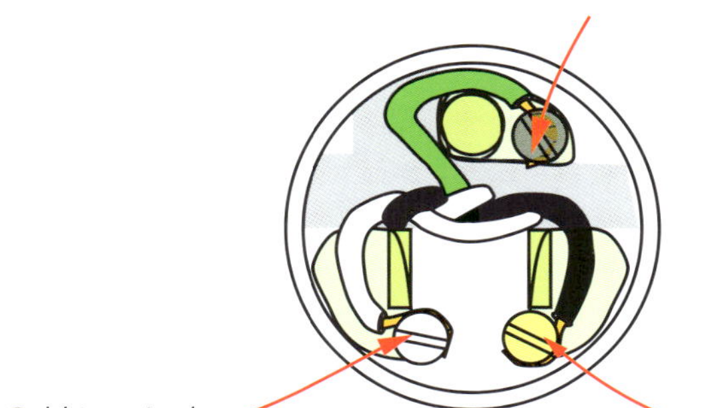

fig. 5

used for. In the USA extension cords should be at least 16 AWG or larger, i.e. 14 AWG or 12 AWG.

- Power strips/sockets should have a built in circuit breaker.

- If making up extension leads never use solid core cable, cord is made from braided wire and is flexible.

16/2 AWG	13A	0 – 50 ft
	10A	50 – 100 ft
16/3 AWG	13A	0 – 50 ft
	10A	50 – 100 ft
14/3 AWG	15A	0 – 50 ft
	13A	50 – 100 ft
12/3AWG	15A	0 – 100 ft
10/3AWG	15A	0 – 100 ft

- A 14 AWG cord should allow for a wide range of equipment use, without the risk of overloading.

(See also Extension Leads and Cable Management, pages 173–179.)

WIRE CONNECTORS

Wire nuts/twist on connectors, are commonly used to connect two or more wires, rather than terminal blocks. They are made to be used by hand and are generally plastic with a metal cone insert that threads and secures the cable. They come in a variety of sizes, rated for the gauge and number of wires being joined. They are colour coded, but this varies with the manufacturer.

Any connections made by this method should be contained either within the appliance or a junction box.

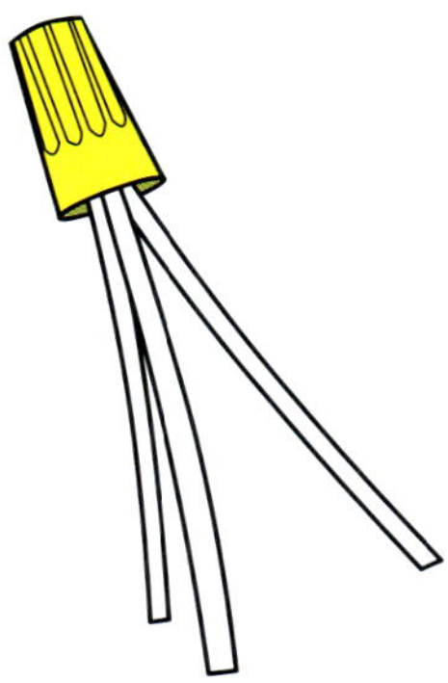

Wire nut

USEFUL WEBSITES

4D modelshop Ltd
www.modelshop.co.uk
Model making materials.

Alec Tiranti Ltd
www.tiranti.co.uk
Sculpture tools and materials suppliers.

Absolute Museum and Gallery Products Ltd
www.absoluteproduct.com
Specialist museum/gallery fixtures.

Aplix Fasteners UK Ltd
www.aplix.co.uk
Velcro manufacturer.

Fischer Fixings (UK) Ltd
www.fischer.co.uk
Fixings manufacturer.

Atlantis
www.atlantis.co.uk
Artists' materials.

Axminster Power Tool Centre Ltd
www.axminster.co.uk
Tools, etc. (good catalogue).

Bighead Bonding Fasteners Ltd
www.bighead.co.uk
Specialist fixings.

Chandlery World
www.chandleryworld.co.uk
Boat-related products.

Falkiner Fine Papers Ltd (now Shepherds Bookbinders Ltd)
www.falkiners.com
Art paper suppliers.

Flint Hire & Supply Ltd
www.flints.co.uk
Theatre ironmongery, tools, rigging, etc.

Ironmongery Direct
www.ironmongerydirect.co.uk
Ironmongery.

Lion Picture Framing Supplies Ltd
www.lionpic.co.uk
Framing and hanging.

MITES – the Moving Image Touring & Exhibition Services
www.fact.co.uk
Specialists in media technology for galleries.

Plasplugs Limited
www.plasplugs.com
Fixings.

www.projectorcentral.com
Projector site, containing a useful guide to calculating projection throws.

Rawlplug Ltd
www.rawlplug.co.uk
Fixings.

Screwfix Direct
www.screwfix.com
Fixings, tools, etc. – particularly good for screws.

Snap-on
www.snapon.com
Tools.

Toolbank
www.toolbankexpress.com
Their catalogue is available nationwide in a large number of builder's merchants.

Tower
www.towerman.co.uk
Fixings, particularly electrical.

GLOSSARY

Acid-free Conservation-grade materials that will not degrade or affect other materials. Normally refers to paper products.

Adaptor block A single electrical plug with multiple sockets to take several plugs.

Allen key A hexagonal key used for tightening or undoing bolts and screws with hex heads. Usually sold in metric or imperial sets.

Anchor fixings A cavity-wall fixing.

Anodise A chemical process to apply a corrosion resistant finish to metal, most commonly aluminium.

Arbour A drill attachment for hole saws.

Aspect ratio The relationship between the height and width of an image.

AV Audiovisual.

Barrel grips A type of cable grip.

Battens Lengths of wood, e.g. split batten.

Bayonet fitting A 'twist and click' fitting.

Blu-ray An optical disc for storage and playback of High Definition data, it will store substantially more than a DVD disc.

BNC (male and female) Video leads.

Bottle screws Another name for straining screws, used for adjusting wire cable.

Bradawl A tool with a sharp point for making small holes in wood.

Breaking load A load which when applied will cause failure of the material.

Bulldog clip A spring clip used for gripping paper.

Burnt disc The term used when information has been copied onto CD or DVD discs.

Cable clip A clip used to secure electrical cable/flex.

Cable tie A plastic tie used to secure electrical flex and other things.

Carbine hook A D-shaped snap hook for use in rigging.

Carousel A tray for housing photographic slides.

Chemical bolt A bolt that uses a resin to bond into a hole.

Chipboard Sheet wood made from compressed chips.

Chocolate block A plastic connecting block for electrical flex.

Chuck Part of the drill that holds the drill bit in place. Chucks tend to be keyless these days, although some drills still have a chuck key for tightening and loosening the bit.

Combi-drill The name given to a cordless drill with a combined function of drilling and hammer action (for masonry use).

Conduit A pipe used for running and covering electric cable.

Contrast ratio This measures the blackest black to the whitest white; the greater the ratio the greater the contrast.

Countersink A bit used for cutting the recess for countersunk screws.

Crimp (ferrule) A soft-metal barrel, used in making loops in cable. Also known as a ferrule or swage.

Crimping tool For use with a crimp.

Cross dowels A bolt fitting.

CRT A cathode ray tube, the old-type television/monitor screen.

Data adaptor For changing from one type of data lead to another.

DLP Digital Light Processing. Projector technology that uses tiny mirrors.

DMD Digital Micro-mirror Device, as DLP.

Dresser hook A right-angled hook.

Duplex grip A different type of cable grip.

DVD Digital Video/Versatile Disc. An optical disc used for storage and playback of data.

DVI Digital Visual Interface. A data lead/connector for high-quality images or data.

Earth A grounding lead used in electrics.

Epoxy A two-part resin, used as a glue.

Ferrules (crimp) A soft metal tube used for making loops in rigging, instead of using a cable grip.

FireWire IEEE 1394 interface. A high-speed data lead typically used in video.

Flange A rim or a rib.

Flex A flexible electrical wire that uses braided rather than solid cable.

Fluorescent light A type of light bulb, originally used in tube form but now also used in compact form for low-energy lighting.

Foamex board Lightweight mounting/display board.

Forstner bit A drill bit for drilling large flat holes in wood.

Gaffer tape Heavy-duty cloth-backed plastic tape.

Gripper gloves Gloves that have a latticework of latex.

Hacksaw A saw with a replaceable blade for cutting metal.

Halogen light High-intensity light.

Hammer-action drill A drill with a hammer function for masonry use.

Hanging bar For hanging unframed work.

HDMI High-Definition Multimedia Interface. A compact audio/video connector.

Hex key See Allen key.

Hole saw A drill attachment for making a large hole. Used with an arbour.

HSS High Speed Steel. A drill bit for use with metal, wood or plastic.

Jack (mono, stereo and mini) Audio lead connector.

Keystone function A projector function for correcting the trapezoid image that occurs when a projector is not centred.

Linen tape Acid-free conservation tape for strengthening and hinging paper works.

Lip & spur bit Drill bit for accurate work in wood.

Live Terminal or wire within electric cable/flex.

Lumen A measurement of light intensity.

Mapping pin A pin with a large head.

Marking gauge A tool for accurate marking of measurements on wood.

Masonry A term that describes brick or concrete walls, floors and ceilings.

MDF Medium Density Fibreboard. Wooden board composed of compressed wood fibre held together using either formaldehyde or non-formaldehyde glue, the latter being preferable for health and safety reasons.

Mini DVI See DVI.

Mini VGA See VGA.

Mini-trunking A channel for running electrical cable.

Mitre joint A cut 45-degree joint, two of which would form a 90-degree corner.

Monitor A video/data screen.

Mylar A polyester film.

Neutral Terminal or wire within electric cable/flex.

Nut spinner Similar in shape to a screwdriver but with a recessed socket end, used for tightening and loosening nuts.

Panel pin A small headless nail.

PAT testing Portable Appliance Testing, a method of ascertaining the safety of electrical equipment.

Pendant light A hanging light fitting.

Perspex Acrylic sheet, available in clear, opaque and coloured forms. Also known as Plexiglas.

Phono An audiovisual lead, mainly for audio but can also be used for video.

Pinion A gearing system, e.g. as used in a hand drill.

Pixels From digital imaging, the smallest piece of information the image is constructed from.

Plasma screen A flat panel screen comprised of tiny gas-filled cells that emit light to produce an image.

Plasterboard Sheet material composed of a plaster sandwich between thin paper/cardboard, used for boarding out internal walls.

Plexiglas See Perspex.

Plumb line A line (string) to which a 'bob' or weight is attached, used for assessing whether something is vertical.

Ply Abbreviation for plywood. Wooden board constructed from layers of thin sheets compressed and glued together.

Ratchet A mechanical device that controls rotational movement, found in ratchet screwdrivers and socket drivers.

Rawlbolt Heavy-duty fixing used in masonry for carrying heavy loads.

Rawlplug A plastic fixing used for light or medium loads in masonry.

RCD Residual Current Device, a safety device for electrical items that cuts the supply in case of failure.

Rigging A method of hanging using cable and/or rope.

Rigging screws Another name for straining screws, used for adjusting or tensioning wire cable.

Router A high-speed cutting tool that will take a range of profiled cutting bits.

S-Video A video lead, now little used, that carries the data as two separate signals (though it does not usually carry the audio signal).

SDS drill and bits A highly efficient masonry drill using a different type of chuck. One that accepts SDS bits, which have a bayonet fastening.

Shackle A connecting device used in rigging.

Shank The part of the screw without a thread. Many screws do not have a shank these days, with the thread going right up to the head.

Shield-anchor bolt A type of Rawlbolt.

Socket driver A tool for holding a range of sockets, used for tightening or loosening nuts.

Solid core cable Electric cable used for permanent installations. It should not be used for temporary installations.

Split battens A hanging device.

Spring toggles Cavity-wall fixings.

Sprocket holes Holes on the edge of film that engage with the camera and/or film projector.

Stanley knife A sharp utility knife known generically in some parts of the world by the name of a firm that makes their own version.

Sticky fixer A small sticky pad – not recommended!

Straining screw Used for adjusting or tensioning wire cable. Also known as bottle or rigging screws and turnbuckles.

Straphanger A hanging device for heavy 2-dimensional work.

Stretcher A frame or support for canvas or material.

Stud detector A device for detecting the studding in plasterboard walls.

Studding (1) A long threaded rod.

Studding (2) The structure for internal walls to which plasterboard, etc. is attached. Can be wood or metal.

Swage See Crimp.

Synched The ability of two or more devices, e.g. DVDs, to start and run consecutively.

Teflon strips Teflon is a low-friction material that enables objects to slide easily.

Thimble A U-shaped channel for making loops in braided wire.

Throw The distance from a projector to the projected image.

Torque A measurement of rotational force.

TPI or PPI Teeth Per Inch or Points Per Inch – measurements of the number of teeth or points in a saw blade.

Try square A tool for marking or checking right angles (90 degrees).

Turnbuckles Used for adjusting or tensioning wire cable. Also known as straining, bottle and rigging screws.

U-bolt A U-shaped bolt with a thread on both ends, as in cable grips.

Universal fixings A term given by some manufacturers to plastic plug fixings that they claim are multifunctional.

USB A high-speed data lead used in video/data.

Velcro A hook and loop fastening, which consists of two strips of material: one covered with tiny hooks, the other with tiny loops. When pressed together the two strips will bond. Often used as an alternative to zips in clothing, but can be equally effective as a hanging, fixing device.

VGA A data lead often used between a computer and projector or monitor.

Vice A device normally found mounted on a workbench for holding objects and materials in place for cutting, drilling, etc.

Webbing A flat length of strong material used for securing items.

Wire stoppers An attachment for wire cable to keep objects in place, e.g. shelves.

Workmate A portable/foldable workbench made by Black & Decker, sometimes used as a generic term for this piece of equipment. It also has an integral vice.

Yankee A type of screwdriver which has both a ratchet and a spiral action. Extremely efficient, the yankee was much used before the advent of cordless drills and screwdrivers, and is still a useful tool to have.

ADDITIONAL NOTES:

ADDITIONAL NOTES:

ADDITIONAL NOTES:

ADDITIONAL NOTES:

ADDITIONAL NOTES: